2024 - 2025

0 POINT
Weight Loss Cookbook

for Beginners

A No-Stress, Mouthwatering and Delicious Recipes to Lose Extra Weight in 365 Days

28 Day
Meal Plan + Dietary Info Included

Laurie Schiffman

Copyright © 2024 Laurie Schiffman
All Right Reserved

Printed in the United States of America

No part of this publication may be reproduced, distributed, or transmitted in any form or by any means, including photocopying, recording, or other electronic or mechanical methods, without the prior written permission of the author, except in the case of brief quotations embodied in critical reviews and specific other noncommercial uses permitted by copyright law.

Table of Contents

PAGE 01
INTRODUCTION

The Science Behind Zero-Point Eating
How to Use this Book?

PAGE 05
THE BREAKFAST

Bundt Cake Breakfast
Flourless Banana Pancakes
Easy Cheeseburger Pie
Bacon and Egg Cucumber Bites
Pineapple Coconut Oatmeal Muffins
Smoked Salmon and Cucumber Rolls
Peanut Butter Energy Balls
Egg Muffins
2-Minute Omelet in a Mug
Hard-Boiled Eggs and Asparagus
Apple Cinnamon Porridge
Turkey Lettuce Wraps
Crispy Air Fryer Turkey Bacon
Zucchini Noodles with Tomato Sauce
French Toast
Cauliflower Rice Porridge
Pumpkin Banana Greek Yogurt Muffins
Burrito Bowl with Spiced Butternut Squash
Grilled Eggplant and Tomato Stack
Instant Pot Egg Bake

PAGE 25
MAIN COURSE

Two-ingredient Dough
Grilled Chicken Salad
Spicy Black Bean Soup
Cauliflower Steak
Zucchini and Carrot Noodles
Caesar Salad
Cabbage Rolls
Eggplant and Tomato Layer Bake
Roasted Mixed Vegetables
Chicken Salad
Chicken and Vegetable Soup
Shrimp and Asparagus Stir-Fry
Stuffed Bell Peppers
Herb-Crusted Pork Tenderloin
Balsamic Glazed Brussels Sprouts
Chicken Piccata
Beef & Bean Chili
Spaghetti Squash with Marinara
Tuna and White Bean Salad

PAGE 45
DINNER

Baked Cod with Tomato and Basil
Chinese Chicken Salad
Slow Cooker Chicken Fajita Soup
Fish Taco Bowls
Mushroom Stroganoff
Chicken Taco Casserole
Quiche
Spaghetti Squash Lasagna
Portobello Mushroom Pizzas
Baked Chicken Parmesan
Beef and Vegetable Kebabs
Lemon and Herb Shrimp
Mushroom Pork Chops
Baked Garlic Lemon Salmon
Baked Buffalo Chicken Taquitos
Chicken Quesadillas
Chickpea and Feta Salad
Southwest Chicken Salad

PAGE 61
SNACKS

Protein Bistro Boxes
Easy Cucumber Chips
Two-ingredient Dough
Instant Pot Premier Protein Yogurt
Sunshine Salad
Baked Sweet Potato Chips
Tofu Chips
Red Lentil Crepes
Roasted Garbanzo Beans
Two Ingredient Pumpkin Muffins
Zero Point Banana Soufflé
No Bake Brownies Without Added Sugar
White Popcorn Kernels
Frozen Grapes
Cabbage Soup
Pickle Wraps
Hashbrown Potatoes
Shrimp Cocktail
White Chicken Chili
Mexican Zero Point Soup

PAGE 81
VEGETARIAN

Vegetable Soup
Zucchini Noodle Caprese
Super-easy Slow-Cooker Three-Bean Chili
Easy Fried Rice
Grilled Cheddar Cheese Sandwiches with Pickles
Tomato Basil Soup
Broccoli & Cheddar Quiche
Grilled Summer Vegetables
Fresh Vegetable Soup
Roasted Mixed Vegetables
Cucumber Noodle Salad
Grilled Asparagus with Lemon
Carrot and Apple Slaw
Stir-Fried Bok Choy
Mushroom and Spinach Saute

PAGE 97
DESSERT

Chocolate Chip Cookies
Chilled Watermelon Soup
Banana Bread
Banana Ice Cream
Berry and Lime Parfait
No Sugar - Less Ghee Churma Ladoo
Peaches with Cinnamon
Non-fat Vanilla Yogurt with Nutmeg
Orange Segments with Cinnamon
Baked Cinnamon Apples
Fruit Salad with Mint
Poached Pears
Healthy Homemade Snack Bar
No Sugar - No Jaggery Dry Fruit Roll
No Atta Banana Halwa

PAGE 112
CONCLUSION

PAGE 113
BONUS

28-Day Meal Plan
Measurement Conversion

Introduction

Imagine starting your day with a hearty breakfast of fluffy pancakes or savoring a creamy bowl of spaghetti squash and marinara for dinner, all without the worry of counting calories or restrictive portions. This was a revelation for me, and perhaps, like many, you've found yourself at a similar crossroads. A few years ago, I stumbled upon the concept of a *"0 point"* diet while navigating through a maze of unsuccessful weight loss attempts, each one leaving me more disheartened than the last. I was on the verge of giving up, believing that a sustainable, enjoyable diet was out of reach. That was until I discovered the transformative power of the *"0 point"* weight loss approach.

The *"0 point"* weight loss diet fundamentally shifts how we think about dieting. Traditionally, weight management strategies have focused on strict calorie counting and an often punishing regimen of what not to eat. However, the "0 point" approach turns this model on its head. It is built on the principle that some foods, primarily wholesome, nutrient-dense foods, can be consumed in generous quantities without sabotaging weight loss goals. These foods are assigned zero points, meaning they do not count towards your daily food point total—an incredibly liberating approach to dieting.

This concept resonates deeply in today's health-conscious society, where the emphasis is increasingly on long-term lifestyle changes rather than short-term diets. The "0 point" diet promotes eating patterns that not only encourage weight loss but also nourish the body. It supports the idea that we should fill our plates with foods that are both nutritious and satisfying—fruits, vegetables, lean proteins, and certain whole grains—allowing for a healthier relationship with food and eating.

The relevance of this diet today cannot be overstated. With obesity rates climbing and health-related diseases such as diabetes and heart disease on the rise, the need for sustainable, health-promoting eating habits is more urgent than ever. The "0 point" diet is not just about losing weight; it's about gaining health. It's a diet that teaches moderation and balance, encouraging individuals to eat until they are satisfied, using foods that fuel the body without adding to the calorie load.

This cookbook, **"0 Point Cookbook for Beginners,"** is crafted with the beginner in mind, providing a guiding light on your journey to a healthier you. It demystifies the "0 point" diet, explaining its foundations and how to incorporate it into your everyday life effortlessly. The recipes you will find here are not only healthy and easy to prepare but also bursting with flavor. We believe that diet food doesn't have to be bland or boring, and this cookbook aims to prove just that.

Each recipe is designed to be straightforward, using common ingredients that promote health without requiring hours in the kitchen. From quick breakfasts and hearty main courses to satisfying snacks and decadent desserts, each dish adheres strictly to the "0 point" guidelines, ensuring that you can enjoy a variety of tastes and textures without any guilt.

Welcome to the world of "0 point" eating—where health meets flavor and your weight loss journey is filled with as much abundance as it is with zest. Let's cook, eat, and celebrate a life of zero deprivation and maximum satisfaction!

The Science Behind Zero-Point Eating

The rationale for designating certain foods as Zero Point is grounded in nutritional science. These foods typically have a low energy density but high nutrient density, meaning they provide a substantial amount of essential nutrients without a high calorie count. This quality makes them ideal for weight management and health improvement, as they can be consumed in larger quantities without leading to weight gain.

The science behind this approach is also focused on metabolic health. Foods high in fiber, lean proteins, and complex carbohydrates, which are common in the Zero Point category, help stabilize blood sugar levels, reduce cholesterol, and maintain satiety longer. This aids in preventing the spikes and dips in energy levels that can lead to overeating.

Furthermore, the psychological benefits of Zero Point eating should not be underestimated. The freedom from counting every calorie helps mitigate the diet fatigue that many experience with more restrictive eating plans. This can lead to more sustainable eating habits, as individuals do not feel trapped by their diet and are more likely to adhere to healthy eating practices in the long term.

In addition, the inclusion of Zero Point foods encourages a more intuitive approach to eating. It aligns with principles of mindful eating, which advocate for listening to one's hunger cues and eating until satiety rather than adhering to strict portion sizes. This approach not only supports physical health but also promotes a healthier psychological relationship with food.

Zero Point eating is not just about promoting weight loss but about encouraging a healthier lifestyle. It supports individuals in making healthy food choices, which contributes to overall well-being and disease prevention. By integrating Zero Point foods into daily meals, individuals can enjoy a varied diet that supports heart health, digestive health, and overall metabolic balance, reinforcing the foundation for a long-term healthy lifestyle.

How to Use this Book?

This book is designed to be your guide to a healthier lifestyle, offering a collection of recipes that are not only delicious but also zero points. Whether you are new to dieting or looking for ways to maintain your health goals without sacrificing flavor, this book is for you.

Before starting any of the recipes, take a moment to familiarize yourself with the concept of zero-point foods. These are items that do not count towards your daily point total on the weight loss plan, helping you stay on track without constant counting or measuring. The introduction section of this book explains which foods qualify as zero-point and offers tips on incorporating them into your diet effectively.

The book is organized into sections based on meal type—breakfast, main courses, dinners, snacks, and desserts. Each recipe is clearly labeled with preparation and cooking times, serving sizes, and a detailed list of ingredients. Instructions are straightforward and easy to follow, ensuring that even beginners can create satisfying meals with ease.

To make the most of this cookbook, consider planning your meals in advance. This approach not only saves time but also helps you balance your meals throughout the day. Each week, select recipes that fit your schedule and preferences, and prepare a shopping list based on the ingredients needed. Some recipes are quick and perfect for busy weekdays, while others may be more suited for leisurely weekend cooking.

Lastly, use this cookbook as a stepping stone to a healthier lifestyle. Engage with the process of cooking and eating mindfully. Share your meals with family or friends and observe the impact of good nutrition on your overall well-being. Don't hesitate to repeat favorites and experiment with new dishes as you grow more confident in your cooking. Remember, every meal is an opportunity to nourish your body and delight your palate.

With the "0 Point Weight Loss Cookbook," you're not just following recipes; you're embarking on a journey of health and flavor. Enjoy the process and the delicious outcomes!

CHAPTER 1

BREAKFAST

2-Minute Omelet in a Mug

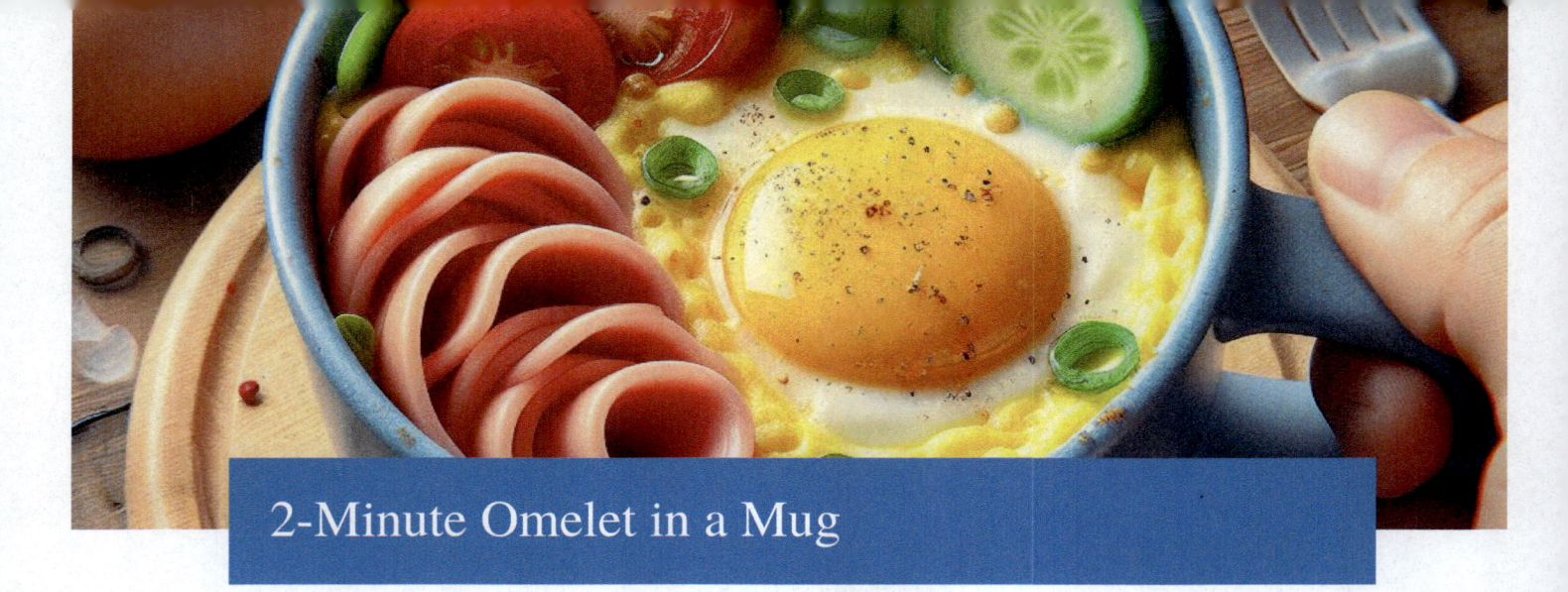

SERVINGS: 1
PREP. TIME: 1 min
COOKING TIME: 1 min 30 sec
DIFFICULTY: Easy

DESCRIPTION

Whip up a quick, nutritious, and low-calorie breakfast with this 2-Minute Egg Omelet in a Mug. It's a straightforward recipe that combines fresh ingredients in a single cup for a delicious start to your day!

INGREDIENTS

- Cooking spray
- 2 eggs
- 1 tablespoon diced roasted red peppers
- 1/4 cup spinach
- 1 tablespoon feta cheese
- 1 teaspoon sliced green onions
- Pepper to taste

DIRECTIONS

1. Coat the inside of a coffee mug with cooking spray.
2. Crack the eggs into the mug and beat them until the yolks and whites are mixed.
3. Add roasted red peppers, spinach, feta cheese, green onions, and a dash of pepper.
4. Stir the mixture gently.
5. Microwave on high for 1 minute and 30 seconds.
6. Let the mug sit for 1 minute before serving.
7. Enjoy your meal!

DIETARY INFO

Calories	187		Carbs	3g
Fat	13g		protein	14g
Fiber	2g			

0 Point Weight Loss Cookbook for Beginners

Pineapple Coconut Oatmeal Muffins

SERVINGS
1 muffin

PREP. TIME
15 min

COOKING TIME
20 min

DIFFICULTY
Easy

DESCRIPTION

These easy-to-make muffins are light, flavorful, and perfect for a nutritious breakfast or snack. Packed with oats, pineapple, and coconut, they're a delightful treat.

INGREDIENTS

- 1 cup rolled oats
- 1/2 cup non-fat Greek yogurt
- 1/2 cup crushed pineapple, drained
- 1/4 cup shredded unsweetened coconut
- 1/4 cup skim milk
- 1 egg
- 1 teaspoon vanilla extract
- 1/2 teaspoon baking powder
- 1/4 teaspoon salt

DIRECTIONS

1. Set the oven to 375°F (190°C). Line a muffin pan with paper liners or grease the cups lightly.
2. In a mixing bowl, combine the oats, Greek yogurt, crushed pineapple, shredded coconut, and skim milk.
3. Stir in the egg and vanilla extract until the mixture is well blended.
4. Add the baking powder and salt, mixing just until incorporated.
5. Spoon the batter into the prepared muffin pan, filling each cup about three-quarters full.
6. Bake for 20 minutes, or until the tops are golden and a toothpick inserted into the center of a muffin comes out clean.
7. Let the muffins cool in the pan and serve.

DIETARY INFO

Calories	98	
Fat	2g	
Fiber	2g	
Carbs	16g	
protein	4g	

Bundt Cake Breakfast

SERVINGS
1 slice

PREP. TIME
10 min

COOKING TIME
25 min

DIFFICULTY
Easy

DESCRIPTION

This Bundt Cake made with nutritious ingredients and a touch of sweetness, it's perfect for a satisfying start to your day without the guilt.

INGREDIENTS

- 1 cup chopped ham
- 2 cups frozen potato nuggets
- 12 eggs, beaten
- 1 can (8 ounces) of biscuit dough, chopped
- 2 cups grated cheddar cheese

DIRECTIONS

1. Set the oven to 400 degrees Fahrenheit.
2. Grease a Bundt pan and set it aside.
3. In a large bowl, combine the ham, potato nuggets, beaten eggs, chopped biscuit dough, and cheddar cheese.
4. Spoon the batter into the Bundt pan that has been oiled. Put in the oven, then bake for forty-five minutes.
5. Once baked, invert the Bundt pan onto a serving platter, slice, and serve.

DIETARY INFO

Calories	260		Carbs	4g
Fat	2g		protein	19g
Fiber	0.1g			

0 Point Weight Loss Cookbook for Beginners

Crispy Air Fryer Turkey Bacon

SERVINGS	**PREP. TIME**	**COOKING TIME**	**DIFFICULTY**
2 slice	5 min	10 min	Easy

DESCRIPTION

It's a quick, straightforward method to enjoy a lower-fat version of crispy bacon, perfect for adding to breakfast plates or garnishing salads and sandwiches.

INGREDIENTS

- 8 slices of turkey bacon

DIRECTIONS

1. Set the temperature of your air fryer to 360°F.
2. Put the turkey bacon pieces in the air fryer basket in a single layer. You may need to do this in batches depending on the size of your air fryer.
3. Cook for 10 minutes, flipping the bacon halfway through the cooking time, until it reaches your desired level of crispiness.
4. Remove the turkey bacon from the air fryer and place it on paper towels to drain any excess fat.

DIETARY INFO

Calories	70		Carbs	0g
Fat	5g		protein	6g
Fiber	0g			

Turkey Lettuce Wraps

SERVINGS
1 wrap

PREP. TIME
10 min

COOKING TIME
15 min

DIFFICULTY
Easy

DESCRIPTION

These wraps use lean ground turkey and fresh vegetables, all nestled in crisp lettuce leaves, making them a delicious part of a zero-point weight loss diet.

INGREDIENTS

- 1 tablespoon olive oil
- 1 pound ground turkey
- 2 cloves garlic, minced
- 1 diced onion
- 1/4 cup hoisin sauce
- 2 tablespoons soy sauce
- 1 tablespoon rice wine vinegar
- 1 tablespoon freshly grated ginger
- 1 teaspoon Sriracha sauce
- 1 (8 ounce) can of water chestnuts, drained and finely chopped
- 2 green onions, thinly sliced
- 1 head of romaine lettuce, leaves separated

DIETARY INFO

Calories	340		Carbs	30g
Fat	13g		protein	27g
Fiber	6g			

DIRECTIONS

1. In a saucepan, warm the olive oil over medium-high heat. Add the ground turkey and cook until it is thoroughly browned, about 3-5 minutes. Be sure to break the turkey into small pieces as it cooks; drain any excess fat.

2. Mix in the minced garlic, diced onion, hoisin sauce, soy sauce, rice wine vinegar, ginger, and Sriracha. Cook until the onions are clear and soft, about 1-2 minutes.

3. Add the chopped water chestnuts and sliced green onions to the pan. Once everything is well blended and heated through, cook for a further one to two minutes, adding more salt & pepper to taste.

4. Serve by spooning a few tablespoons of the turkey mixture into the center of a lettuce leaf and wrap it like a taco.

Apple Cinnamon Porridge

SERVINGS
1

PREP. TIME
5 min

COOKING TIME
15 min

DIFFICULTY
Easy

DESCRIPTION

This Apple Cinnamon Porridge is made with wholesome ingredients, it's a zero-point recipe that's both filling and delicious.

INGREDIENTS

- 1 medium apple, peeled and diced
- 1/2 cup rolled oats
- 1 cup water
- 1/2 teaspoon ground cinnamon
- 1/4 teaspoon nutmeg
- Sweetener of choice to taste (optional)

DIRECTIONS

1. In a small saucepan, combine the diced apple, rolled oats, water, cinnamon, and nutmeg.
2. Bring the mixture to a boil over medium heat, then reduce the heat to low and simmer for about 10-15 minutes, or until the porridge is thick and creamy. Stir occasionally to prevent sticking.
3. Taste and add sweetener if desired, mixing thoroughly to combine.
4. Serve the porridge hot, with additional cinnamon sprinkled on top if desired.

DIETARY INFO

Calories	200	Carbs	38g
Fat	3g	protein	5g
Fiber	6g		

Smoked Salmon and Cucumber Rolls

SERVINGS	PREP. TIME	COOKING TIME	DIFFICULTY
2 rolls	10 min	0 min	Easy

DESCRIPTION

Smoked Salmon and Cucumber Rolls are a refreshing and elegant appetizer or snack that combines the rich flavor of smoked salmon with the crisp freshness of cucumber

INGREDIENTS

- 100g smoked salmon, thinly sliced
- 1 large cucumber
- 1 tablespoon light cream cheese
- Fresh dill or chives for garnish
- Lemon wedges for serving

DIRECTIONS

1. Wash the cucumber and use a vegetable peeler or mandoline to slice it lengthwise into thin strips.
2. Place a cucumber slice on a level surface. If using, spread a thin layer of cream cheese over the cucumber slice.
3. Place a slice of smoked salmon on top of the cucumber, add a sprig of dill or a few chives, and carefully roll up the cucumber tightly.
4. Repeat with the remaining ingredients until all the cucumber slices and salmon are used.
5. Serve the rolls immediately with lemon wedges on the side for squeezing over the rolls.

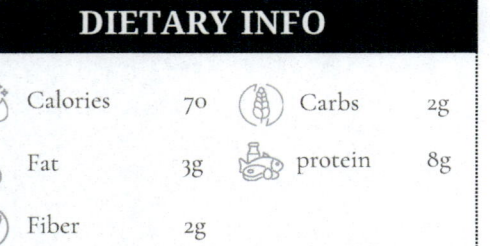

DIETARY INFO

Calories	70		Carbs	2g
Fat	3g		protein	8g
Fiber	2g			

0 Point Weight Loss Cookbook for Beginners

Bacon and Egg Cucumber Bites

SERVINGS
4

PREP. TIME
15 min

COOKING TIME
10 min

DIFFICULTY
Easy

DESCRIPTION

Bacon and Egg Cucumber Bites offer a delightful and health-conscious twist on traditional breakfast flavors, combining crispy bacon, creamy eggs, and fresh cucumber in a bite-sized snack.

INGREDIENTS

- 1 large cucumber
- 4 slices turkey bacon
- 4 eggs
- Fresh chives, finely chopped (for garnish)
- Salt and pepper to taste

DIETARY INFO

Calories	90	Carbs	2g
Fat	5g	protein	8g
Fiber	1g		

DIRECTIONS

1. In a pan over medium heat, cook the turkey bacon until crispy. Set aside on a paper towel to drain and cool. Once cool, chop into small pieces.
2. Hard boil the eggs: Place eggs in a saucepan and cover with water. Bring to a boil, then cover, remove from heat, and let stand for 8-10 minutes. Rinse under cold water and peel. Chop the eggs finely.
3. Wash the cucumber and cut into thick slices (about 3/4-inch thick). Using a small spoon or melon baller, scoop out the center of each cucumber slice to create a small cup, being careful not to pierce through the bottom.
4. In a bowl, mix the chopped eggs with the crumbled bacon, add salt and pepper to taste, and stir to combine.
5. Spoon the bacon and egg mixture into the hollowed-out cucumber slices. Garnish each bite with chopped chives.
6. Serve immediately, or chill in the refrigerator until serving.

Easy Cheeseburger Pie

SERVINGS
1 slice

PREP. TIME
15 min

COOKING TIME
25 min

DIFFICULTY
Easy

DESCRIPTION

This recipe is a simple, savory pie that combines lean meat, cheese, and a light crust, making it a satisfying meal without the guilt.

INGREDIENTS

- 150g lean ground beef (95% lean)
- 1/2 cup chopped onion
- 1 clove garlic, minced
- 1/2 teaspoon salt
- 1/4 teaspoon pepper
- 1/2 cup shredded reduced-fat cheddar cheese
- 1/2 cup Greek yogurt
- 1/2 cup water
- 2 eggs
- 1/2 cup whole wheat flour
- 1 teaspoon baking powder

DIETARY INFO

Calories 220
Carbs 15g
Fat 8g
protein 23g
Fiber 2g

DIRECTIONS

1. Set the oven's temperature to 400°F, or 200°C. Grease a 9-inch pie plate very lightly.
2. In a skillet over medium heat, cook the ground beef, onion, and garlic until the beef is thoroughly browned and the onions are soft. Drain any excess grease. Add pepper and salt to the mixture to season it.
3. Spread the cooked beef evenly in the bottom of the prepared pie plate. Sprinkle the shredded cheese over the meat.
4. In a mixing bowl, whisk together the Greek yogurt, water, eggs, whole wheat flour, and baking powder until smooth. Pour this mixture over the cheese and beef in the pie plate.
5. Bake in the preheated oven for 25 minutes, or until the center is set and the edges are golden brown.
6. Let the pie cool for 5 minutes before slicing and serving.

Grilled Eggplant and Tomato Stack

SERVINGS	PREP. TIME	COOKING TIME	DIFFICULTY
1 stack	15 min	10 min	Easy

DESCRIPTION

This recipe features the smoky flavor of grilled eggplant paired with the fresh taste of ripe tomatoes, accented by fresh basil and a drizzle of balsamic glaze, making it perfect for a light lunch or a side dish.

INGREDIENTS

- 1 medium eggplant, sliced into 1/2 inch rounds
- 2 large ripe tomatoes, sliced
- Fresh basil leaves
- Salt and pepper to taste
- Balsamic glaze (optional)

DIRECTIONS

1. Turn the heat up to medium-high on your grill or grill pan.
2. Add salt and pepper to the eggplant slices for seasoning. Grill the eggplant slices for about 3-4 minutes on each side, until they are tender and have grill marks.
3. Assemble the stack by placing a slice of grilled eggplant on a plate, followed by a slice of tomato and a basil leaf. Repeat the layering until all ingredients are used up, finishing with a slice of tomato.
4. Drizzle the stack with balsamic glaze if using, and season with additional salt and pepper to taste.
5. Serve immediately, enjoying the blend of flavors and textures.

DIETARY INFO

Calories	120	Carbs	27g
Fat	1g	protein	3g
Fiber	9g		

0 Point Weight Loss Cookbook for Beginners

Cauliflower Rice Porridge

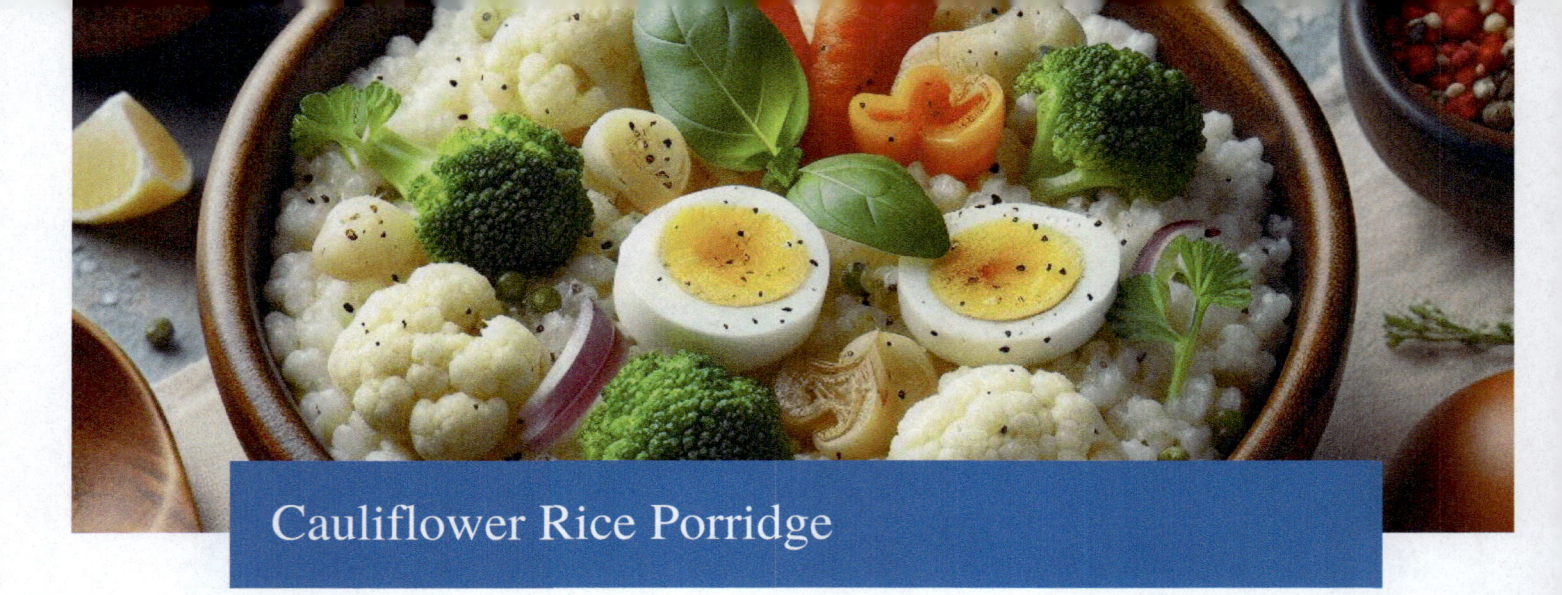

SERVINGS
1 bowl

PREP. TIME
5 min

COOKING TIME
10 min

DIFFICULTY
Easy

DESCRIPTION

This dish is made from cauliflower rice, infused with flavors that make it both nourishing and satisfying, all within the guidelines of a zero-point weight loss plan.

INGREDIENTS

- 1 cup riced cauliflower
- 1/2 cup unsweetened almond milk
- 1 tablespoon chia seeds
- 1/2 teaspoon cinnamon
- 1/4 teaspoon vanilla extract
- Sweetener of choice to taste (optional)
- Fresh berries for topping (optional)

DIRECTIONS

1. In a small saucepan, combine the riced cauliflower, almond milk, chia seeds, cinnamon, and vanilla extract.
2. Cook over medium heat, stirring frequently, until the mixture is heated through and begins to thicken, about 8-10 minutes.
3. Remove from heat and stir in your preferred sweetener if desired.
4. Serve the porridge warm, topped with fresh berries if using.

DIETARY INFO

Calories	100	Carbs	12g
Fat	5g	protein	3g
Fiber	6g		

Zucchini Noodles with Tomato Sauce

SERVINGS 1
PREP. TIME 10 min
COOKING TIME 20 min
DIFFICULTY Easy

DESCRIPTION

This dish pairs the light, crisp texture of spiralized zucchini with a robust and flavorful homemade tomato sauce, offering a satisfying meal that's both nutritious and filling.

INGREDIENTS

- 2 medium zucchinis, spiralized into noodles
- 1 tablespoon olive oil
- 1/2 cup chopped onion
- 2 garlic cloves, minced
- 1 cup crushed tomatoes
- 1 teaspoon dried basil
- 1 teaspoon dried oregano
- Salt and pepper to taste
- Fresh basil for garnish (optional)

DIETARY INFO

Calories	180	Carbs	27g
Fat	7g	protein	4g
Fiber	6g		

DIRECTIONS

1. In a big skillet over medium heat, warm the olive oil. Add the chopped onion and minced garlic, and sauté until the onion becomes translucent, about 5 minutes.
2. Stir in the crushed tomatoes, dried basil, and oregano. Season with salt and pepper. Reduce the heat and let the sauce simmer for 10 minutes to blend the flavors.
3. Make the zucchini noodles while the sauce is simmering. Place the spiralized zucchini in a colander and sprinkle with a little salt to draw out excess moisture. Let sit for a few minutes, then gently squeeze the noodles to remove water.
4. Add the zucchini noodles to the sauce in the skillet. Toss gently to coat the noodles with the sauce and cook for about 5 minutes, or until the zucchini is tender but still al dente.
5. Serve the noodles hot, garnished with fresh basil if desired.

0 Point Weight Loss Cookbook for Beginners

Peanut Butter Energy Balls

SERVINGS 1 ball | **PREP. TIME** 15 min | **COOKING TIME** 0 min | **DIFFICULTY** Easy

DESCRIPTION

These no-bake energy balls are packed with protein and fiber, making them ideal for a quick energy boost during the day or a post-workout treat.

INGREDIENTS

- 1/2 cup natural peanut butter (unsweetened and unsalted)
- 1 cup old-fashioned oats
- 2 tablespoons honey (optional)
- 1/4 cup ground flaxseed
- 2 tablespoons chia seeds
- 1 teaspoon vanilla extract
- 1/2 teaspoon cinnamon
- 1/4 cup mini chocolate chips (optional)

DIRECTIONS

1. In a large bowl, combine the peanut butter, oats, honey, ground flaxseed, chia seeds, vanilla extract, and cinnamon. Stir until all ingredients are well mixed. If the mixture seems too dry, add a little more peanut butter to help it bind.
2. Fold in the mini chocolate chips, if using.
3. Using a spoon, scoop out the dough and form into small balls, about 1 inch in diameter. Place each ball on a baking sheet lined with parchment paper.
4. Chill the energy balls in the refrigerator for at least 30 minutes to set, which makes them easier to handle.
5. Store the energy balls in an airtight container in the refrigerator for up to a week or freeze for longer storage.

DIETARY INFO

- Calories: 100
- Fat: 6g
- Fiber: 2g
- Carbs: 9g
- protein: 3g

Egg Muffins

SERVINGS	PREP. TIME	COOKING TIME	DIFFICULTY
1 muffin	10 min	20 min	Easy

DESCRIPTION

Egg Muffins are a savory, protein-packed breakfast option that's easy to make and perfect for on-the-go mornings.

INGREDIENTS

- 6 large eggs
- 1/2 cup diced bell peppers (any color)
- 1/2 cup chopped spinach
- 1/4 cup diced onions
- Salt and pepper to taste
- Non-stick cooking spray

DIRECTIONS

1. Set the oven temperature to 190°C. Spray a muffin tin with non-stick cooking spray to prevent sticking.
2. In a large bowl, whisk the eggs until the yolks and whites are well combined.
3. Stir in the diced bell peppers, chopped spinach, and diced onions into the egg mixture. Season with salt and pepper.
4. Pour the egg mixture evenly into the muffin tin cavities, filling each about two-thirds full.
5. Bake in the preheated oven for 20 minutes, or until the muffins are set in the middle and slightly golden on top.
6. Remove from the oven and let cool for a few minutes before removing from the muffin tin. Serve warm.

DIETARY INFO

- Calories: 70
- Fat: 4g
- Fiber: 1g
- Carbs: 2g
- protein: 6g

Flourless Banana Pancakes

SERVINGS: 2 pancakes
PREP. TIME: 5 min
COOKING TIME: 10 min
DIFFICULTY: Easy

DESCRIPTION

Perfect for a quick morning meal, these pancakes are naturally sweetened with bananas, making them a healthy choice for anyone on a weight loss journey.

INGREDIENTS

- 2 ripe bananas
- 2 large eggs
- 1/2 teaspoon cinnamon
- Non-stick cooking spray or a drop of olive oil for cooking

DIRECTIONS

1. In a mixing bowl, mash the ripe bananas with a fork until smooth.
2. Crack the eggs into the bowl with the mashed bananas and add the cinnamon and vanilla extract. Whisk the mixture until it is well combined and slightly frothy.
3. Heat a non-stick skillet over medium heat and lightly grease it with cooking spray or a drop of olive oil.
4. Pour small circles of batter onto the hot skillet (about 1/4 cup for each pancake). Cook for about 2-3 minutes on one side until you see bubbles forming on the surface, then flip carefully and cook for another 1-2 minutes on the other side until golden brown and cooked through.
5. Serve the pancakes warm. Optional toppings include fresh fruit or a zero-point sweetener.

DIETARY INFO

Calories	160	Carbs	27g
Fat	5g	protein	6g
Fiber	3g		

0 Point Weight Loss Cookbook for Beginners

Hard-Boiled Eggs and Asparagus

SERVINGS	PREP. TIME	COOKING TIME	DIFFICULTY
1	5 min	15 min	Easy

DESCRIPTION

Hard-Boiled Eggs and Asparagus is a simple, elegant dish that pairs the mild flavors of eggs with the earthy tones of asparagus

INGREDIENTS

- 2 large eggs
- 10 spears of asparagus, trimmed
- Salt and pepper to taste
- Optional: vinegar or lemon juice for poaching asparagus

DIRECTIONS

1. Place the eggs in a saucepan and cover them with cold water by an inch. Bring over high heat to a boil. Once boiling, cover the pan and remove it from the heat. Let stand for 12 minutes.
2. While the eggs are cooking, prepare the asparagus. In a another pot, bring some water to a boil. You can add a little vinegar or lemon juice if you like. Add the asparagus and cook until tender yet firm, about 2-4 minutes depending on the thickness.
3. Drain the asparagus and plunge it into ice water to stop the cooking process and maintain its bright green color.
4. After 12 minutes, transfer the eggs to a bowl of ice water to cool.
5. Once cool, peel the eggs and slice them in half.
6. Arrange the cooked asparagus on a plate. Top with the halved hard-boiled eggs. Season with salt and pepper to taste.

DIETARY INFO

Calories	160	Carbs	4g
Fat	10g	protein	13g
Fiber	2g		

Pumpkin Banana Greek Yogurt Muffins

SERVINGS 1 | **PREP. TIME** 15 min | **COOKING TIME** 20 min | **DIFFICULTY** Easy

DESCRIPTION
These muffins are perfect for a quick breakfast or a guilt-free snack, fitting seamlessly into a zero-point weight loss plan.

INGREDIENTS

- 1 medium ripe banana, mashed
- 1/2 cup pure pumpkin puree
- 1/2 cup non-fat Greek yogurt
- 1/4 cup honey (optional)
- 1 large egg
- 1 cup whole wheat flour
- 1/2 teaspoon baking soda
- 1/2 teaspoon baking powder
- 1 teaspoon cinnamon
- 1/2 teaspoon nutmeg
- 1/4 teaspoon salt

DIETARY INFO
- Calories 95
- Fat 1g
- Fiber 3g
- Carbs 18g
- Protein 4g

DIRECTIONS

1. Turn the oven on to 375°F, or 190°C. Use paper liners or nonstick cooking spray to line a muffin pan.
2. In a large bowl, combine the mashed banana, pumpkin puree, Greek yogurt, and honey (if using). Blend well, mixing fully. Add the egg and stir until combined.
3. In a separate bowl, whisk together the whole wheat flour, baking soda, baking powder, cinnamon, nutmeg, and salt.
4. Gradually add the dry ingredients to the wet ingredients, stirring just until the flour is incorporated. Avoid overmixing to keep the muffins light and fluffy.
5. The batter should be poured into the muffin tin, about three-quarters of the way up each cup.
6. Bake for 20 minutes, or until a toothpick inserted into the center of a muffin comes out clean.
7. After the muffins have cooled in the pan for five minutes, move them to a wire rack to finish cooling.

Burrito Bowl with Spiced Butternut Squash

SERVINGS: 1 bowl
PREP. TIME: 15 min
COOKING TIME: 30 min
DIFFICULTY: Easy

DESCRIPTION
This hearty bowl features roasted butternut squash, black beans, and fresh vegetables, topped with zesty seasonings. It's a perfect meal for anyone looking for a satisfying, low-point option in their diet.

INGREDIENTS

- 1 cup butternut squash, peeled and cubed
- 1/2 teaspoon olive oil
- 1 teaspoon chili powder
- 1/2 teaspoon cumin
- Salt and pepper to taste
- 1/2 cup cooked black beans, rinsed and drained
- 1/2 cup cooked brown rice
- 1/4 cup diced tomatoes
- 1/4 cup chopped red onion
- 1/4 cup chopped cilantro
- Lime wedges for serving

DIRECTIONS

1. Set the oven to 400°F (200°C). Toss the cubed butternut squash with olive oil, chili powder, cumin, salt, and pepper. Spread on a baking sheet and roast for 25-30 minutes, or until tender and slightly caramelized.
2. While the squash is roasting, prepare the other components. Arrange the cooked brown rice in the bottom of a bowl.
3. Top the rice with cooked black beans, diced tomatoes, and roasted butternut squash.
4. Sprinkle chopped red onion and cilantro over the top.
5. Serve with lime wedges on the side, and if desired, add sliced avocado or a spoonful of salsa on top.

DIETARY INFO

- Calories: 350
- Carbs: 65g
- Fat: 5g
- protein: 10g
- Fiber: 12g

Instant Pot Egg Bake

SERVINGS	PREP. TIME	COOKING TIME	DIFFICULTY
1	10 min	20 min	Easy

DESCRIPTION

Using an Instant Pot, this recipe combines eggs with a mix of vegetables and spices, creating a flavorful, zero-point meal that's perfect for starting your day or enjoying as a protein-packed snack.

INGREDIENTS

- 4 large eggs
- 1/2 cup chopped spinach
- 1/4 cup diced bell peppers
- 1/4 cup chopped mushrooms
- 1/4 cup diced onions
- Salt and pepper to taste
- Non-stick cooking spray or a little olive oil for greasing

DIRECTIONS

1. Grease the inside of a 7-inch round baking dish that fits inside your Instant Pot with non-stick cooking spray or a little olive oil.
2. In a bowl, beat the eggs with a whisk until well mixed. Add the chopped spinach, bell peppers, mushrooms, and onions to the eggs.
3. Secure the lid of the Instant Pot and set it to "Manual" or "Pressure Cook" high for 15 minutes.
4. When the cooking time is complete, allow a natural pressure release for 5 minutes, then manually release any remaining pressure before opening the lid.
5. Carefully remove the baking dish from the Instant Pot, remove the foil, and let the egg bake cool slightly before serving.

DIETARY INFO

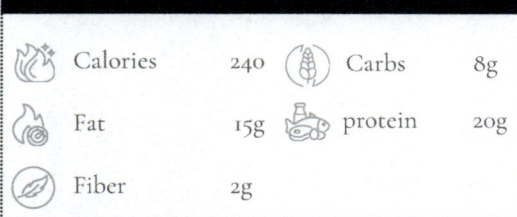

Calories	240	Carbs	8g
Fat	15g	protein	20g
Fiber	2g		

0 Point Weight Loss Cookbook for Beginners

CHAPTER 2

MAIN COURSES

Grilled Chicken Salad

SERVINGS 1 | **PREP. TIME** 15 min | **COOKING TIME** 15 min | **DIFFICULTY** Easy

DESCRIPTION
This Grilled Chicken Salad is a light, refreshing meal that combines the smoky flavor of grilled chicken with crisp vegetables and a zesty dressing.

INGREDIENTS

- 150g chicken breast, boneless and skinless
- Salt and pepper to taste
- Mixed salad greens (lettuce, spinach, arugula, etc.)
- 1/2 cucumber, sliced
- 1/2 bell pepper, thinly sliced
- 1/4 red onion, thinly sliced
- 1 tablespoon balsamic vinegar
- 1 teaspoon Dijon mustard
- 1 teaspoon lemon juice
- Non-stick cooking spray

DIETARY INFO

Calories	230	Carbs	12g
Fat	6g	protein	26g
Fiber	3g		

DIRECTIONS

1. Turn the heat up to medium-high on the grill. Season the chicken breast with salt and pepper. Spray lightly with non-stick cooking spray to prevent sticking.
2. Grill the chicken for about 7-8 minutes on each side, or until fully cooked through and juices run clear. An internal temperature should reach 165°F (74°C). Remove from the grill and let it rest for a few minutes before slicing thinly.
3. In a large mixing bowl, combine the mixed salad greens, sliced cucumber, bell pepper, and red onion.
4. In a small bowl, whisk together the balsamic vinegar, Dijon mustard, and lemon juice to make the dressing. Add more salt and pepper to taste.
5. Include the salad with the cooked chicken slices. Pour the dressing over the salad and gently toss to ensure that all of the items are uniformly coated.
6. Serve the salad immediately, ensuring a mix of greens, vegetables, and chicken in each portion.

0 Point Weight Loss Cookbook for Beginners

Cabbage Rolls

SERVINGS	**PREP. TIME**	**COOKING TIME**	**DIFFICULTY**
2 rolls	20 min	45 min	Moderate

DESCRIPTION

These Cabbage Rolls are a hearty, flavorful German dish and its a non-starch veggie that fits perfectly into a zero-point weight loss plan.

INGREDIENTS

- 8 large cabbage leaves
- 150g ground turkey (low fat)
- 1/2 cup chopped onion
- 1 clove garlic, minced
- 1/2 cup grated carrots
- 1/2 cup finely chopped mushrooms
- 1 cup diced tomatoes (canned or fresh)
- 1/2 teaspoon dried oregano
- 1/2 teaspoon dried basil
- Salt and pepper to taste
- 1 cup low sodium chicken or vegetable broth

DIETARY INFO

Calories	240	Carbs	18g
Fat	7g	protein	28g
Fiber	6g		

DIRECTIONS

1. Start by boiling a big kettle of water. Blanch the cabbage leaves for about 2-3 minutes, or until softened. Drain and set aside to cool.
2. Cook the ground turkey in a skillet over medium heat until it's no longer pink. Add onion, garlic, carrots, and mushrooms, cooking until the vegetables are soft, about 5-7 minutes.
3. Stir in half of the diced tomatoes, oregano, basil, salt, and pepper. Cook for an additional 5 minutes until everything is well combined.
4. Preheat your oven to 350°F (175°C).
5. Lay out the cabbage leaves on a flat surface. Place a portion of the turkey and vegetable mixture onto the center of each leaf. To enclose the filling, fold in the sides and roll up the leaf. Secure with toothpicks if necessary.
6. Place the rolls seam side down in a baking dish. Pour the remaining diced tomatoes and broth over the top.
7. Cover with foil and bake in the preheated oven for about 30 minutes.
8. Uncover and bake for an additional 15 minutes, or until the cabbage is tender and the filling is heated through.

Spicy Black Bean Soup

SERVINGS
1 bowl

PREP. TIME
10 min

COOKING TIME
20 min

DIFFICULTY
Easy

DESCRIPTION

This Spicy Black Bean Soup is a robust, flavorful dish packed with fiber from black beans and is seasoned with a blend of spices to give it a hearty kick.

INGREDIENTS

- 1 cup canned black beans, rinsed and drained
- 1/2 cup chopped onion
- 1 garlic clove, minced
- 1/2 cup chopped red bell pepper
- 2 cups low sodium vegetable broth
- 1 tsp chili powder
- 1/2 tsp cumin
- 1/4 tsp cayenne pepper (adjust to taste)
- Salt and pepper to taste
- 1 tbsp chopped cilantro for garnish
- Juice of 1/2 lime

DIRECTIONS

1. In a large pot over medium heat, sauté onions, garlic, and red bell pepper until onions are translucent, about 5 minutes.
2. Add black beans, vegetable broth, chili powder, cumin, and cayenne pepper. Bring to a boil.
3. Reduce heat to low and simmer for 15 minutes, allowing the flavors to meld.
4. Use an immersion blender to partially blend the soup for a thicker consistency, leaving some beans whole for texture.
5. Season with salt and pepper to taste. Stir in lime juice.
6. Serve hot, garnished with chopped cilantro.

DIETARY INFO

Calories	210	Carbs	3g
Fat	1g	protein	12g
Fiber	9g		

0 Point Weight Loss Cookbook for Beginners

Chicken and Vegetable Soup

SERVINGS	PREP. TIME	COOKING TIME	DIFFICULTY
1 bowl	10 min	30 min	Easy

DESCRIPTION

This Chicken and Vegetable Soup is a comforting and hearty dish, perfect for any season. Packed with lean protein from chicken and loaded with nutritious vegetables, this soup is flavorful, and filling.

INGREDIENTS

- 150g chicken breast, cut into bite-sized pieces
- 1/2 cup chopped onion
- 1 garlic clove, minced
- 1/2 cup chopped carrots
- 1/2 cup chopped celery
- 1/2 cup diced tomatoes
- 3 cups low sodium chicken broth
- 1 tsp dried thyme
- 1 tsp dried parsley
- Salt and pepper to taste
- Non-stick cooking spray

DIRECTIONS

1. Spray a large pot with non-stick cooking spray and heat over medium heat. Add the chicken pieces and cook until lightly browned on all sides.
2. Add onions, garlic, carrots, and celery to the pot. Sauté for about 5 minutes, or until the vegetables start to soften.
3. Pour in the diced tomatoes and chicken broth. Stir in thyme and parsley.
4. Bring the soup to a boil, then reduce heat and simmer for about 20 minutes, or until the vegetables are tender and the chicken is fully cooked.
5. To taste, add salt and pepper for seasoning.
6. Present heated, topped with more parsley if preferred.

DIETARY INFO

Calories	250		Carbs	25g
Fat	3g		protein	30g
Fiber	6g			

Zucchini and Carrot Noodles

SERVINGS 1   **PREP. TIME** 15 min   **COOKING TIME** 10 min   **DIFFICULTY** Easy

DESCRIPTION

Zucchini and Carrot Noodles are a vibrant, nutritious alternative to traditional pasta, perfect for anyone looking to reduce carbohydrate intake while still enjoying flavorful and satisfying meals.

INGREDIENTS

- 1 large zucchini
- 2 large carrots
- 1 tablespoon olive oil
- 1/2 cup cherry tomatoes, halved
- 1 garlic clove, minced
- Salt and pepper to taste
- 1/4 teaspoon red pepper flakes (optional)
- Fresh herbs like basil or parsley for garnish

DIRECTIONS

1. Use a spiralizer or a vegetable peeler to turn the zucchini and carrots into noodles. Set aside.
2. In a big skillet over medium heat, warm up the olive oil. Add the minced garlic and red pepper flakes, if using, and sauté for about 1 minute until fragrant.
3. Add the cherry tomatoes to the skillet and cook for about 3 minutes until they start to soften and release their juices.
4. Add the zucchini and carrot noodles to the skillet. Toss well to coat with the garlic and tomato mixture. Cook for about 5-7 minutes, stirring occasionally, until the noodles are tender but still have a slight crunch.
5. To taste, add salt and pepper for seasoning.
6. Garnish with fresh herbs and serve hot.

DIETARY INFO

Calories	180	Carbs	27g
Fat	7g	protein	3g
Fiber	6g		

Shrimp and Asparagus Stir-Fry

SERVINGS: 1
PREP. TIME: 10 min
COOKING TIME: 10 min
DIFFICULTY: Easy

DESCRIPTION

Shrimp and Asparagus Stir-Fry is a light, vibrant dish that combines succulent shrimp and crisp asparagus with flavorful seasonings, making it a perfect quick and healthy meal.

INGREDIENTS

- 150g shrimp, peeled and deveined
- 1 cup asparagus, trimmed and cut into 1-inch pieces
- 1 tablespoon olive oil
- 2 cloves garlic, minced
- 1 teaspoon ginger, minced
- 1 tablespoon low sodium soy sauce
- 1/2 teaspoon sesame oil
- Salt and pepper to taste
- Optional: Sesame seeds for garnish

DIRECTIONS

1. Heat the olive oil in a large skillet or wok over medium-high heat.
2. Add the minced garlic and ginger to the pan and sauté for about 30 seconds, just until fragrant.
3. Add the shrimp to the pan and stir-fry for about 2 minutes, or until they start to turn pink.
4. Add the asparagus pieces and continue to stir-fry for another 5-7 minutes, until the asparagus is tender-crisp and the shrimp are fully cooked.
5. Drizzle the soy sauce and sesame oil over the shrimp and asparagus. Toss everything together for it to coat well. Season with salt and pepper to taste.
6. Serve immediately, garnished with sesame seeds if desired.

DIETARY INFO

Calories	250	Carbs	10g
Fat	10g	protein	28g
Fiber	3g		

Roasted Mixed Vegetables

SERVINGS 1 | **PREP. TIME** 10 min | **COOKING TIME** 30 min | **DIFFICULTY** Easy

DESCRIPTION

This roasted mixed vegetables recipe offers a colorful, nutrient-rich side dish that pairs well with any main course. Featuring a variety of vegetables, this dish is seasoned with herbs and spices.

INGREDIENTS

- 1/2 cup carrots, peeled and sliced
- 1/2 cup zucchini, sliced
- 1/2 cup bell peppers, assorted colors, chopped
- 1/2 cup broccoli florets
- 1/2 cup cauliflower florets
- 2 tablespoons olive oil
- 1 teaspoon garlic powder
- 1 teaspoon dried thyme
- Salt and pepper to taste

DIRECTIONS

1. Set your oven to 400°F (200°C).
2. In a large bowl, combine the sliced carrots, zucchini, chopped bell peppers, broccoli, and cauliflower florets.
3. Drizzle the vegetables with olive oil and sprinkle with garlic powder, thyme, salt, and pepper. Toss well to ensure all the vegetables are evenly coated.
4. Spread the vegetables in a single layer on a baking sheet.
5. Roast in the preheated oven for about 30 minutes, stirring halfway through, until the vegetables are tender and slightly caramelized.
6. Remove from the oven and serve immediately or allow to cool and store for later use.

DIETARY INFO

Calories 200 | Carbs 18g
Fat 14g | protein 4g
Fiber 6g

0 Point Weight Loss Cookbook for Beginners

Cauliflower Steak

SERVINGS	PREP. TIME	COOKING TIME	DIFFICULTY
1 steak	10 min	25 min	Easy

DESCRIPTION

Cauliflower Steak is a delicious, hearty, and healthy alternative to traditional steaks. Perfect for vegetarians or those looking to reduce meat consumption

INGREDIENTS

- 1 large head of cauliflower
- 2 tablespoons olive oil
- 1 teaspoon garlic powder
- 1 teaspoon smoked paprika
- Salt and pepper to taste
- Fresh parsley, chopped for garnish

DIRECTIONS

1. Set the oven temperature to 400°F, or 200°C.
2. Take off the cauliflower's leaves and thin out the stem, making sure the head stays whole.
3. Cut the cauliflower vertically into steaks that are 1 inch thick. Depending on the size of your cauliflower, you can get about 2 to 3 good steaks from the middle portion (the outer slices might fall apart but can be roasted alongside).
4. In a small bowl, mix the olive oil, garlic powder, smoked paprika, salt, and pepper.
5. Brush both sides of each cauliflower steak with the oil and spice mixture.
6. Place the cauliflower steaks on a baking sheet lined with parchment paper.
7. Roast in the preheated oven for about 25 minutes, flipping halfway through, until the cauliflower is tender and the edges are crispy and browned.
8. Serve hot, garnished with fresh parsley.

DIETARY INFO

Calories	160	Carbs	15g
Fat	10g	protein	5g
Fiber	7g		

0 Point Weight Loss Cookbook for Beginners

Two-ingredient Dough

SERVINGS 2 - 3 | **PREP. TIME** 5 min | **COOKING TIME** 20 min | **DIFFICULTY** Easy

DESCRIPTION

This Two-ingredient Dough recipe is a versatile and simple base that can be used for a variety of dishes such as pizzas, flatbreads, and pastries.

INGREDIENTS

- 1 cup self-rising flour (To make zero points, use a zero-point flour alternative like oat or chickpea flour)
- 1 cup non-fat Greek yogurt

DIRECTIONS

1. In a mixing bowl, combine the self-rising flour and non-fat Greek yogurt. Stir with a fork until the mixture starts to come together.
2. Turn out the dough onto a lightly floured surface (use the same zero-point flour if necessary). Knead the dough for about 5 to 8 minutes, until it becomes smooth and elastic. If the dough is too sticky, gradually add a little more flour as you knead.
3. Once kneaded, the dough is ready to be shaped according to your recipe needs. It can be rolled out for pizza, divided into portions for flatbreads, or used as a base for other recipes.
4. To cook, follow the baking instructions specific to your recipe. For a basic flatbread, bake in a preheated oven at 375°F (190°C) for 18-20 minutes or until golden brown.
5. The dough can also be cooked on a stovetop griddle for about 2-3 minutes on each side if making flatbreads or wraps.

DIETARY INFO

Calories	0		Carbs	0g
Fat	1g		protein	5g
Fiber	0g			

0 Point Weight Loss Cookbook for Beginners

Balsamic Glazed Brussels Sprouts

SERVINGS 1 | **PREP. TIME** 10 min | **COOKING TIME** 20 min | **DIFFICULTY** Easy

DESCRIPTION

This recipe is perfect for anyone looking to add a delicious and healthy option to their meals, suitable for a zero-point weight loss plan.

INGREDIENTS

- 2 cups Brussels sprouts, trimmed and halved
- 1 tablespoon olive oil
- 2 tablespoons balsamic vinegar
- Salt and pepper to taste
- Optional: a pinch of garlic powder for extra flavor

DIRECTIONS

1. Set your oven to 400°F (200°C).
2. In a large bowl, toss the Brussels sprouts with olive oil, salt, and pepper until they are well coated.
3. Arrange the Brussels sprouts on a baking sheet in a single layer. Roast in the preheated oven for about 15-20 minutes, or until they are tender and the edges are caramelized, stirring halfway through for even cooking.
4. Remove from the oven and drizzle the balsamic vinegar over the cooked Brussels sprouts. Toss to coat evenly.
5. If desired, sprinkle a pinch of garlic powder for added flavor, and toss again to distribute the spices.
6. Serve warm as a side dish.

DIETARY INFO

Calories	150	Carbs	20g
Fat	7g	protein	5g
Fiber	6g		

Eggplant and Tomato Layer Bake

SERVINGS 1 | **PREP. TIME** 15 min | **COOKING TIME** 45 min | **DIFFICULTY** Easy

DESCRIPTION

This recipe is perfect for a zero-point meal, offering a deliciously satisfying way to enjoy vegetables in a main course or as a substantial side dish.

INGREDIENTS

- 2 cups Brussels sprouts, trimmed and halved
- 1 tablespoon olive oil
- 2 tablespoons balsamic vinegar
- Salt and pepper to taste
- Optional: a pinch of garlic powder for extra flavor

DIRECTIONS

1. Set your oven to 375°F (190°C). Spray a baking dish with non-stick cooking spray.
2. Arrange a layer of eggplant slices at the bottom of the dish. Overlap if necessary.
3. Sprinkle some of the minced garlic and chopped basil over the eggplant. Season with salt and pepper.
4. Place a layer of tomato slices over the eggplant. Repeat the seasoning with a little more garlic, basil, salt, and pepper.
5. Continue layering eggplant and tomatoes, seasoning each layer, until all ingredients are used.
6. If using, sprinkle the top layer with grated parmesan cheese.
7. Cover with foil and bake in the preheated oven for 30 minutes.
8. Remove the foil and bake for an additional 15 minutes, or until the vegetables are tender and the top is slightly golden.
9. Remove from oven and let it cool for a few minutes before serving.

DIETARY INFO

Calories	180		Carbs	40g
Fat	1g		protein	6g
Fiber	14g			

0 Point Weight Loss Cookbook for Beginners

Caesar Salad

SERVINGS	PREP. TIME	COOKING TIME	DIFFICULTY
1	10 min	0 min	Easy

DESCRIPTION

This recipe maintains the creamy, tangy flavors of a Caesar dressing without the added fats and calories, making it perfect for a healthy, satisfying meal.

INGREDIENTS

- 2 cups romaine lettuce, washed and chopped
- 1/2 cup low-fat Greek yogurt
- 2 anchovy fillets, rinsed and minced (optional)
- 1 clove garlic, minced
- Juice of 1/2 lemon
- 1 teaspoon Worcestershire sauce
- 1 teaspoon Dijon mustard
- Salt and black pepper to taste
- 1 tablespoon grated Parmesan cheese (optional)
- 1 whole wheat pita bread, toasted and cut into pieces for croutons (optional)

DIRECTIONS

1. In a small bowl, combine Greek yogurt, minced anchovies (if using), minced garlic, lemon juice, Worcestershire sauce, and Dijon mustard. Whisk until smooth and well blended. For it to have a taste, add salt and pepper for seasoning.
2. Put the chopped romaine lettuce in a big bowl. Drizzle the dressing over the lettuce and toss well to coat evenly.
3. If using, sprinkle grated Parmesan cheese over the salad and add the toasted whole wheat pita pieces as croutons.
4. Serve immediately, ensuring the lettuce stays crisp and the flavors are fresh.

DIETARY INFO

Calories	70	Carbs	10g
Fat	1g	protein	6g
Fiber	2g		

0 Point Weight Loss Cookbook for Beginners

Herb-Crusted Pork Tenderloin

SERVINGS 1 **PREP. TIME** 10 min **COOKING TIME** 25 min **DIFFICULTY** Easy

DESCRIPTION

This Herb-Crusted Pork Tenderloin is a savory, aromatic main course that's simple to prepare yet impressive enough for special occasions.

INGREDIENTS

- 1 pork tenderloin (approximately 500g)
- 1 tablespoon Dijon mustard
- 1 clove garlic, minced
- 1 teaspoon dried rosemary
- 1 teaspoon dried thyme
- 1/2 teaspoon dried oregano
- Salt and pepper to taste
- Non-stick cooking spray

DIRECTIONS

1. Set your oven to 375°F (190°C).
2. Trim the pork tenderloin of any extra fat. Pat the surface dry with paper towels.
3. In a small bowl, mix together the Dijon mustard, minced garlic, rosemary, thyme, oregano, salt, and pepper to create the herb paste.
4. Rub the herb paste evenly over all sides of the pork tenderloin.
5. Heat a skillet over medium-high heat and spray with non-stick cooking spray. Sear the pork tenderloin on all sides until golden brown, about 2-3 minutes per side.
6. Transfer the pork tenderloin to a roasting pan or baking sheet lined with foil.
7. Roast in the preheated oven for about 20 minutes, or until the internal temperature reaches 145°F (63°C) on a meat thermometer.
8. Take the pork out of the oven, and give it five minutes to rest before slicing. This allows the juices to redistribute throughout the meat, ensuring it stays moist and flavorful.
9. After slicing, present the pork tenderloin.

DIETARY INFO

Calories	220	Carbs	1g
Fat	9g	protein	32g
Fiber	0g		

0 Point Weight Loss Cookbook for Beginners

Stuffed Bell Peppers

SERVINGS
1

PREP. TIME
15 min

COOKING TIME
30 min

DIFFICULTY
Easy

DESCRIPTION

Stuffed Bell Peppers are a colorful and nutritious dish filled with a savory mixture of vegetables and protein.

INGREDIENTS

- 4 bell peppers, tops cut off and seeds removed
- 1 cup ground turkey breast (99% fat-free)
- 1/2 cup finely chopped onion
- 1 clove garlic, minced
- 1 cup chopped mushrooms
- 1 zucchini, finely chopped
- 1 cup canned diced tomatoes, no salt added
- 1 teaspoon dried oregano
- 1 teaspoon dried basil
- Salt and pepper to taste
- 1/2 cup low sodium chicken broth

DIETARY INFO

Calories	150	Carbs	18g
Fat	2g	protein	18g
Fiber	5g		

DIRECTIONS

1. Set your oven to 375°F (190°C).
2. In a skillet over medium heat, cook the ground turkey until fully browned. Add the onions, garlic, mushrooms, and zucchini. Cook until the vegetables are softened, about 5-7 minutes.
3. Stir in the diced tomatoes, oregano, basil, salt, and pepper. Simmer the mixture for another 5 minutes until everything is well combined and slightly reduced.
4. Arrange the bell peppers in a baking dish. Spoon the turkey and vegetable mixture into each bell pepper cavity.
5. Pour the chicken broth into the bottom of the baking dish around the peppers. This will help to keep the peppers moist while they bake.
6. Cover the dish with aluminum foil and bake in the preheated oven for about 25-30 minutes, or until the peppers are tender and the filling is hot.
7. Remove the foil and bake for an additional 5 minutes to allow the tops to brown slightly.
8. Serve the stuffed bell peppers hot.

Chicken Salad

SERVINGS 1 | **PREP. TIME** 15 min | **COOKING TIME** 0 min | **DIFFICULTY** Easy

DESCRIPTION

This Chicken Salad is not only delicious and easy to prepare but also incredibly versatile. You can serve it over a bed of greens, stuffed into a whole wheat pita, or on its own for a satisfying meal.

INGREDIENTS

- 150g cooked chicken breast, shredded or chopped
- 1/2 cup diced celery
- 1/4 cup chopped red onion
- 1/4 cup diced cucumber
- 1/4 cup non-fat Greek yogurt
- 1 tablespoon Dijon mustard
- 1 tablespoon lemon juice
- Salt and pepper to taste
- 1/4 teaspoon paprika (optional)
- Fresh parsley, chopped (for garnish)

DIRECTIONS

1. In a large mixing bowl, combine the shredded chicken, diced celery, chopped red onion, and diced cucumber.
2. In a small bowl, mix the non-fat Greek yogurt, Dijon mustard, lemon juice, salt, pepper, and paprika (if using) until smooth. This will be your dressing.
3. Drizzle the chicken and veggies with the dressing. Toss everything together until well combined and evenly coated with the dressing.
4. Refrigerate the salad for at least 10 minutes to let the flavors meld together, though you can serve it immediately if desired.
5. Serve chilled, garnished with fresh parsley.

DIETARY INFO

Calories	220	Carbs	10g
Fat	3g	protein	35g
Fiber	2g		

Spaghetti Squash with Marinara

SERVINGS	PREP. TIME	COOKING TIME	DIFFICULTY
1	10 min	40 min	Easy

DESCRIPTION

It combines the nutritious, fiber-rich spaghetti squash with a flavorful, homemade marinara sauce for a filling meal that aligns perfectly with a zero-point weight loss plan.

INGREDIENTS

- 1 medium spaghetti squash
- 1 cup low sodium marinara sauce (homemade or store-bought with no added sugar)
- 1 teaspoon olive oil
- 1 clove garlic, minced
- 1/2 cup chopped onion
- 1/2 teaspoon dried basil
- 1/2 teaspoon dried oregano
- Salt and pepper to taste
- Fresh basil, chopped (for garnish)

DIETARY INFO

Calories	180		Carbs	30g
Fat	4g		protein	4g
Fiber	6g			

DIRECTIONS

1. Set your oven to 400°F (200°C).
2. Remove the seeds by slicing the spaghetti squash in half lengthwise. Place the squash halves cut-side down on a baking sheet lined with parchment paper.
3. Bake in the preheated oven for 30-40 minutes, or until the flesh of the squash is tender and can be shredded into spaghetti-like strands with a fork.
4. While the squash is baking, heat the olive oil in a saucepan over medium heat. Add the minced garlic and chopped onion, sautéing until the onion is translucent and fragrant.
5. Add the oregano, basil, marinara sauce, salt, and pepper. Simmer on low heat for about 10 minutes, allowing the flavors to blend together.
6. Once the squash is cooked, remove it from the oven and let it cool slightly before using a fork to scrape the inside to create the "spaghetti" strands.
7. Plate the spaghetti squash and top with the warm marinara sauce.
8. Garnish with fresh basil before serving.

Beef & Bean Chili

SERVINGS
1

PREP. TIME
10 min

COOKING TIME
30 min

DIFFICULTY
Easy

DESCRIPTION

This Beef & Bean Chili combines lean ground beef with fiber-rich beans and a blend of spices for a filling meal that's low in points, making it a great option for those on a weight loss plan.

INGREDIENTS

- 150g lean ground beef (95% lean)
- 1/2 cup chopped onion
- 1 clove garlic, minced
- 1 cup canned diced tomatoes, no salt added
- 1/2 cup low sodium beef broth
- 1/2 cup canned kidney beans, rinsed and drained
- 1 teaspoon chili powder
- 1/2 teaspoon cumin
- 1/2 teaspoon paprika
- Salt and pepper to taste

DIRECTIONS

1. Turn up the heat to medium in a big saucepan. Add the ground beef, breaking it up with a spoon, and cook until browned.
2. Include the minced garlic and chopped onion in the pot with the beef. Cook until the onions are translucent, about 5 minutes.
3. Stir in the diced tomatoes, beef broth, kidney beans, chili powder, cumin, and paprika. Simmer the mixture for a while.
4. Reduce heat to low and let the chili simmer, uncovered, for about 20 minutes to allow the flavors to meld and the chili to thicken. Stir occasionally.
5. Season with salt and pepper to taste.
6. Serve hot, garnished with chopped cilantro or green onions if desired.

DIETARY INFO

Calories	320	Carbs	28g
Fat	8g	protein	35g
Fiber	8g		

0 Point Weight Loss Cookbook for Beginners

Tuna and White Bean Salad

SERVINGS	PREP. TIME	COOKING TIME	DIFFICULTY
1	10 min	0 min	Easy

DESCRIPTION

Tuna and White Bean Salad is a light, refreshing dish that combines protein-rich tuna and fiber-filled white beans with crisp vegetables and a zesty dressing.

INGREDIENTS

- 1 can (about 140g) of tuna in water, drained
- 1 cup canned white beans (such as cannellini), rinsed and drained
- 1/2 cup cherry tomatoes, halved
- 1/4 cup red onion, finely chopped
- 1/4 cup cucumber, diced
- 1 tablespoon chopped fresh parsley
- Juice of 1 lemon
- 1 tablespoon extra virgin olive oil
- Salt and pepper to taste

DIRECTIONS

1. In a large bowl, combine the drained tuna and white beans.
2. Add the cherry tomatoes, red onion, cucumber, and fresh parsley to the bowl.
3. In a small bowl, whisk together the lemon juice, olive oil, salt, pepper, and red pepper flakes (if using) to make the dressing.
4. Pour the dressing over the salad ingredients and gently toss to combine everything evenly.
5. Taste and, if needed, adjust the seasoning.
6. Serve immediately, or chill in the refrigerator for about an hour to allow the flavors to meld together.

DIETARY INFO

Calories	350	Carbs	35g
Fat	10g	protein	25g
Fiber	10g		

0 Point Weight Loss Cookbook for Beginners

Chicken Piccata

SERVINGS 1 | **PREP. TIME** 10 min | **COOKING TIME** 20 min | **DIFFICULTY** Easy

DESCRIPTION
Chicken Piccata is a classic Italian dish that is both simple and elegant. It features chicken breasts cooked in a light lemon-caper sauce, offering a bright and tangy flavor that is both refreshing and satisfying.

INGREDIENTS

- 1 boneless, skinless chicken breast (approximately 150g)
- Salt and pepper to taste
- 1/2 tablespoon olive oil
- 1 clove garlic, minced
- Juice of 1/2 lemon
- 1/2 cup low sodium chicken broth
- 1 tablespoon capers, rinsed
- Fresh parsley, chopped (for garnish)
- Optional: 1 tablespoon unsalted butter or a butter substitute for richness

DIETARY INFO
Calories	350	Carbs	35g
Fat	10g	protein	25g
Fiber	10g		

DIRECTIONS

1. Flatten the chicken breast to an even thickness of about 1/2 inch using a meat mallet or rolling pin. This promotes even cooking of the chicken. Use salt and pepper to season both sides.
2. Heat the olive oil in a skillet over medium-high heat. Once hot, add the chicken breast and cook for about 4-5 minutes on each side, or until golden brown and cooked through. After taking the chicken out of the skillet, set it aside.
3. In the same skillet, add the minced garlic and sauté for about 30 seconds until fragrant.
4. Add the lemon juice and chicken broth to the skillet, bringing the mixture to a boil. Reduce heat and simmer for about 3 minutes, allowing the sauce to reduce slightly.
5. Stir in the capers and optional butter or butter substitute. Cook for an additional 2 minutes, allowing the sauce to thicken slightly.
6. Return the chicken to the skillet and spoon the sauce over the chicken to reheat and coat it thoroughly.
7. Serve the chicken hot, garnished with chopped parsley.

0 Point Weight Loss Cookbook for Beginners

CHAPTER 3

DINNER

Chicken Taco Casserole

SERVINGS 1 | **PREP. TIME** 15 min | **COOKING TIME** 25 min | **DIFFICULTY** Easy

DESCRIPTION

This Chicken Taco Casserole is a comforting, flavorful dish that combines the zesty flavors of a taco in a hearty, baked casserole form.

INGREDIENTS

- 1 cup cooked, shredded chicken breast
- 1/2 cup chopped onions
- 1/2 cup diced bell peppers (mix of colors)
- 1 clove garlic, minced
- 1 cup canned black beans, rinsed and drained
- 1 cup chopped tomatoes
- 1 cup low sodium chicken broth
- 1 tsp chili powder
- 1 tsp cumin
- 1/2 tsp paprika
- Salt and pepper to taste
- 1/2 cup chopped fresh cilantro (for garnish)

DIRECTIONS

1. Preheat the oven to 375°F (190°C).
2. In a large skillet over medium heat, sauté onions, bell peppers, and garlic until they are soft, about 5-7 minutes.
3. Add the shredded chicken, black beans, chopped tomatoes, chicken broth, chili powder, cumin, and paprika to the skillet. After giving it a quick stir, reduce the heat to a simmer.
4. Season with salt and pepper to taste. Cook for an additional 5 minutes, allowing the flavors to meld together.
5. Transfer mixture to an oven-safe dish. If using, sprinkle the reduced-fat shredded cheese over the top.
6. Bake in the preheated oven for 15-20 minutes, or until the casserole is bubbly and the cheese is melted and slightly golden.
7. Take out of the oven and give it a few minutes to cool. Before serving, add some chopped cilantro as a garnish.

DIETARY INFO

Calories	220	Carbs	22g
Fat	3g	protein	28g
Fiber	7g		

0 Point Weight Loss Cookbook for Beginners

Lemon and Herb Shrimp

SERVINGS 1
PREP. TIME 10 min
COOKING TIME 10 min
DIFFICULTY Easy

DESCRIPTION

Lemon and Herb Shrimp is not only delicious and easy to prepare but also highly nutritious. It's an excellent source of protein and provides a boost of flavor without adding extra calories or points.

INGREDIENTS

- 150g fresh shrimp, peeled and deveined
- Juice of 1 lemon
- 1 tablespoon olive oil
- 1 clove garlic, minced
- 1 teaspoon dried parsley
- 1 teaspoon dried basil
- Salt and pepper to taste
- Additional lemon wedges for serving
- Optional: Fresh parsley for garnish

DIRECTIONS

1. In a bowl, combine the lemon juice, olive oil, minced garlic, dried parsley, dried basil, salt, and pepper. Whisk together to create the marinade.
2. Toss the shrimp in the marinade to ensure even coating. Let marinate for about 5-10 minutes (do not marinate for too long as the lemon juice can start to cook the shrimp).
3. Turn the heat up to medium-high in a skillet. Once hot, add the shrimp along with the marinade to the skillet.
4. Cook the shrimp for about 2-3 minutes on each side or until they are pink and fully cooked.
5. Remove from heat and transfer the shrimp to a serving plate. Squeeze additional lemon over the top if desired and garnish with fresh parsley.
6. Serve immediately with lemon wedges on the side for extra zest.

DIETARY INFO

Calories	200		Carbs	3g
Fat	10g		protein	24g
Fiber	0g			

Spaghetti Squash Lasagna

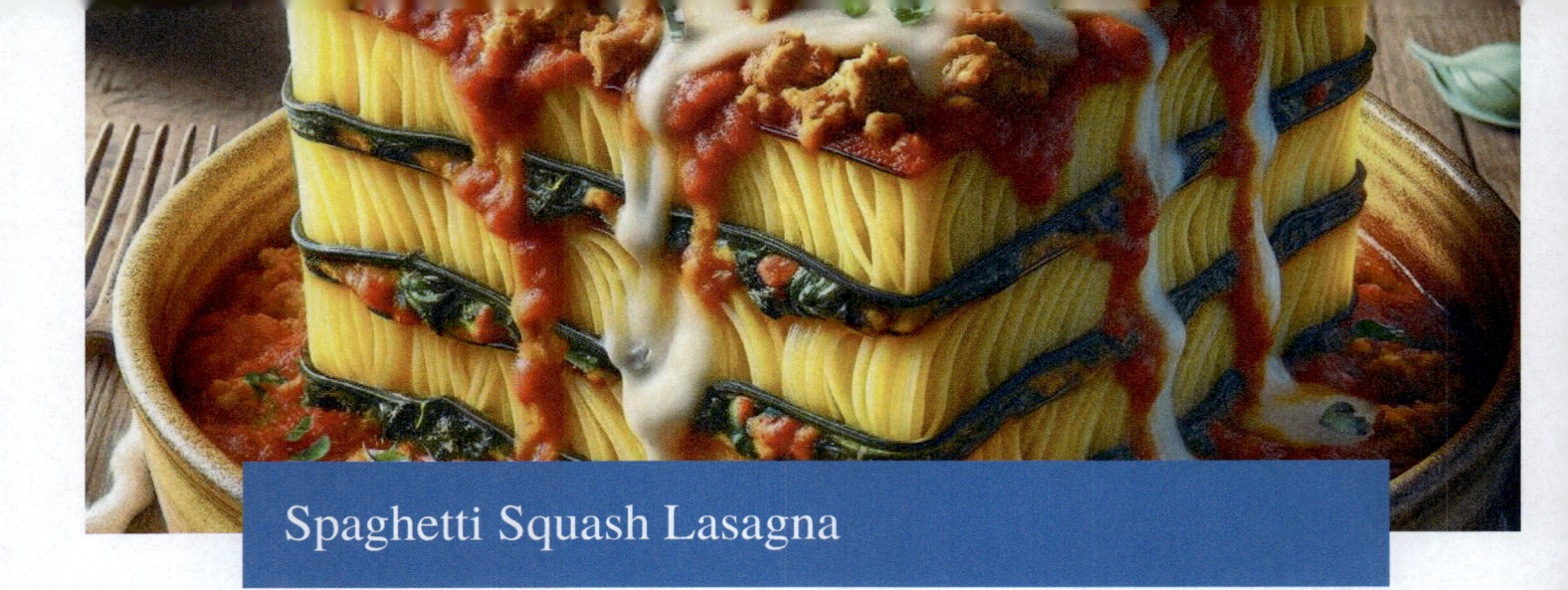

SERVINGS 1   **PREP. TIME** 15 min   **COOKING TIME** 45 min   **DIFFICULTY** Easy

DESCRIPTION

Spaghetti Squash Lasagna layers all the hearty flavors of traditional lasagna with the health benefits of spaghetti squash, making it a fantastic low-carb, zero-point alternative.

INGREDIENTS

- 1 medium spaghetti squash
- 1 cup low-fat ricotta cheese
- 1/2 cup grated Parmesan cheese (optional)
- 1 egg
- 1 cup homemade or low-sodium marinara sauce
- 1/2 cup chopped onions
- 2 cloves garlic, minced
- 1/2 lb ground turkey breast
- 1 teaspoon dried basil
- 1 teaspoon dried oregano
- Salt and pepper to taste
- Fresh basil for garnish

DIETARY INFO

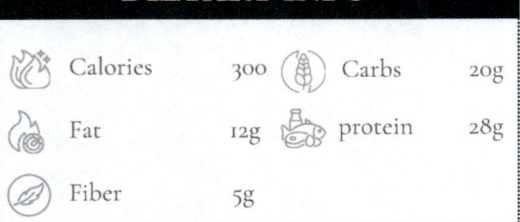

Calories 300   Carbs 20g
Fat 12g   protein 28g
Fiber 5g

DIRECTIONS

1. Set the oven temperature to 400°F, or 200°C.
2. Remove the seeds by slicing the spaghetti squash in half lengthwise. Transfer the squash halves, cut-side down, to a parchment paper-lined baking sheet. Bake for 30-40 minutes, or until the flesh is easily shredded with a fork.
3. Preheat a skillet to medium heat while the squash bakes. Add the ground turkey, onions, and garlic, cooking until the turkey is browned and the onions are soft.
4. Stir in 1/2 cup of marinara sauce, basil, oregano, salt, and pepper. Simmer for about 5 minutes, then remove from heat.
5. In a bowl, mix the ricotta cheese, Parmesan cheese, and egg. Stir until well combined.
6. Once the squash is done, reduce the oven temperature to 375°F (190°C). Use a fork to scrape the inside of the squash to create spaghetti-like strands.
7. In a baking dish, layer half of the spaghetti squash strands. Top with half of the turkey mixture and half of the ricotta mixture. Repeat the layers. Pour the remaining 1/2 cup of marinara sauce over the top.
8. Cover with foil and bake for 20 minutes. Remove the foil and bake for an additional 10 minutes, or until the top is lightly browned and bubbling.
9. Garnish with fresh basil before serving.

0 Point Weight Loss Cookbook for Beginners

Mushroom Stroganoff

SERVINGS	PREP. TIME	COOKING TIME	DIFFICULTY
1	10 min	20 min	Easy

DESCRIPTION

Mushroom Stroganoff is a vegetarian twist on the classic beef stroganoff. This dish features earthy mushrooms in a creamy, savory sauce served over noodles or rice.

INGREDIENTS

- 2 cups sliced mushrooms (such as cremini or button mushrooms)
- 1/2 cup chopped onions
- 2 cloves garlic, minced
- 1 tablespoon olive oil
- 1 cup low-fat or fat-free sour cream (or Greek yogurt for a healthier option)
- 1/2 cup low sodium vegetable broth
- 1 tablespoon Worcestershire sauce
- 1 teaspoon Dijon mustard
- Salt and pepper to taste
- Fresh parsley, chopped (for garnish)

DIETARY INFO

Calories	200		Carbs	20g
Fat	10g		protein	9g
Fiber	3g			

DIRECTIONS

1. In a big skillet over medium heat, warm the olive oil. Add the onions and garlic, sautéing until they begin to soften, about 3-4 minutes.
2. Fill the skillet with the cut mushrooms. Cook, stirring occasionally, until the mushrooms are tender and their juices are released, about 5-7 minutes.
3. Stir in the vegetable broth, Worcestershire sauce, Dijon mustard, and smoked paprika (if using). Bring the mixture to a simmer and cook for about 5 minutes, allowing it to slightly reduce.
4. Reduce the heat to low and stir in the sour cream or Greek yogurt. Mix until the sauce is smooth and heated through but not boiling. To taste, add salt and pepper for seasoning.
5. Serve the mushroom stroganoff over cooked whole wheat noodles or brown rice, garnished with fresh parsley.

0 Point Weight Loss Cookbook for Beginners

Baked Cod with Tomato and Basil

SERVINGS 1 | **PREP. TIME** 10 min | **COOKING TIME** 20 min | **DIFFICULTY** Easy

DESCRIPTION

Baked Cod with Tomato and Basil is a light, flavorful dish that combines tender cod fillets with the fresh tastes of tomato and basil.

INGREDIENTS

- 1 cod fillet (approximately 150g)
- 1/2 cup cherry tomatoes, halved
- 1/4 cup fresh basil leaves, chopped
- 2 cloves garlic, minced
- 1 tablespoon olive oil
- Salt and pepper to taste
- Lemon wedges for serving

DIRECTIONS

1. Set your oven to 400°F (200°C).
2. Place the cod fillet in a baking dish. Season both sides of the cod with salt and pepper.
3. In a bowl, mix together the halved cherry tomatoes, chopped basil, minced garlic, and olive oil.
4. Spoon the tomato and basil mixture over the cod fillet in the baking dish.
5. Bake in the preheated oven for about 15-20 minutes, or until the cod is cooked through and flakes easily with a fork.
6. Serve the baked cod hot, garnished with additional fresh basil and lemon wedges on the side.

DIETARY INFO

Calories	220	Carbs	5g
Fat	12g	protein	23g
Fiber	1g		

Slow Cooker Chicken Fajita Soup

SERVINGS
1

PREP. TIME
15 min

COOKING TIME
6 - 8 hour

DIFFICULTY
Easy

DESCRIPTION

This dish is perfect for those busy days when you want to come home to a ready-to-eat meal that's both satisfying and compatible with a zero-point weight loss plan.

INGREDIENTS

- 1 pound boneless, skinless chicken breasts
- 1/2 cup diced onions
- 1 bell pepper, sliced (any color)
- 2 cloves garlic, minced
- 1 jalapeño, seeded and finely chopped (optional)
- 1 cup low sodium chicken broth
- 1 can (14.5 oz) diced tomatoes, no salt added
- 1 teaspoon chili powder
- 1 teaspoon cumin
- 1/2 teaspoon paprika
- Salt and pepper to taste
- 1/2 lime, juiced
- Fresh cilantro, chopped (for garnish)

DIETARY INFO

Calories	220	Carbs	15g
Fat	3g	protein	28g
Fiber	3g		

DIRECTIONS

1. Place the chicken breasts at the bottom of the slow cooker.
2. Add the diced onions, sliced bell peppers, minced garlic, and chopped jalapeño over the chicken.
3. In a bowl, mix the diced tomatoes (with their juice), chicken broth, chili powder, cumin, paprika, salt, and pepper. Stir to combine.
4. Pour the tomato and spice mixture over the chicken and vegetables in the slow cooker.
5. Cover and cook on low for 6-8 hours or on high for 3-4 hours.
6. Once the cooking time is complete, remove the chicken from the slow cooker and shred it using two forks. Return the shredded chicken to the slow cooker.
7. Stir in the fresh lime juice and adjust seasoning if necessary.
8. Garnish the heated soup with finely chopped fresh cilantro.

Baked Chicken Parmesan

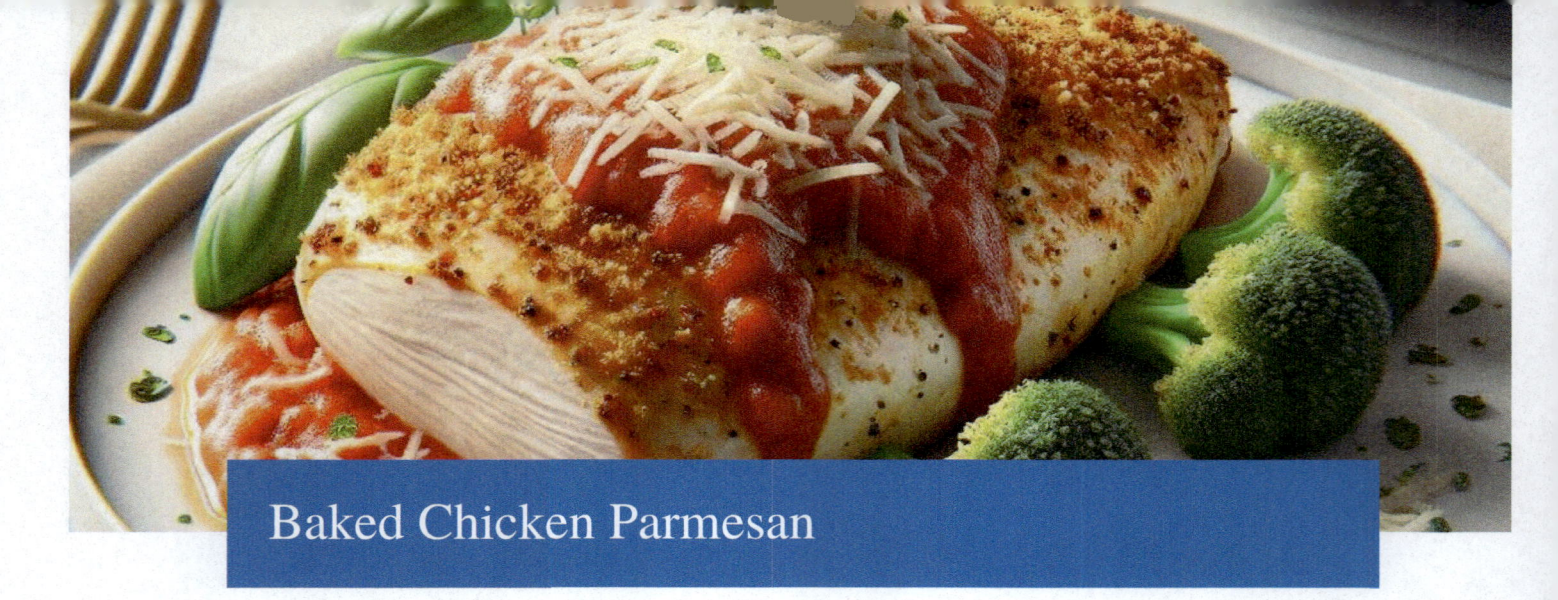

SERVINGS	PREP. TIME	COOKING TIME	DIFFICULTY
1	15 min	25 min	Easy

DESCRIPTION

Baked Chicken Parmesan is a healthier take on the traditional Italian dish, utilizing baking instead of frying to achieve a crispy, flavorful crust without the extra fat.

INGREDIENTS

- 1 boneless, skinless chicken breast (approximately 150g)
- Salt and pepper to taste
- 1/2 cup crushed whole wheat breadcrumbs (or zero-point breadcrumbs if available)
- 1 tablespoon grated Parmesan cheese (optional)
- 1 teaspoon dried Italian herbs (basil, oregano, thyme)
- 1/2 cup low sodium tomato sauce
- 1/2 cup shredded part-skim mozzarella cheese (optional,)
- Non-stick cooking spray
- Fresh basil leaves for garnish

DIETARY INFO

Calories 230
Fat 4g
Fiber 3g
Carbs 18g
protein 28g

DIRECTIONS

1. Set your oven to 375°F (190°C). Line a baking sheet with parchment paper and spray lightly with non-stick cooking spray.
2. Season the chicken breast with salt and pepper.
3. In a shallow dish, mix the crushed breadcrumbs, Parmesan cheese, and dried herbs.
4. Dredge the chicken breast in the breadcrumb mixture, pressing to coat evenly on both sides. Place the coated chicken on the prepared baking sheet.
5. Bake in the preheated oven for 20 minutes, or until the chicken is nearly cooked through and the coating is golden and crisp.
6. Remove from the oven, spoon the tomato sauce over the chicken, and top with shredded mozzarella cheese if using.
7. Return to the oven and bake for an additional 5 minutes, or until the cheese is melted and bubbly and the chicken is fully cooked (internal temperature should reach 165°F or 74°C).
8. Garnish with fresh basil leaves before serving.

0 Point Weight Loss Cookbook for Beginners

Fish Taco Bowls

SERVINGS 1 | **PREP. TIME** 15 min | **COOKING TIME** 15 min | **DIFFICULTY** Easy

DESCRIPTION
They're ideal for a quick lunch or dinner and offer a light, satisfying meal that fits seamlessly into a health-focused diet.

INGREDIENTS

- 150g white fish fillets (such as tilapia or cod)
- 1 teaspoon olive oil
- 1 teaspoon chili powder
- 1/2 teaspoon ground cumin
- Salt and pepper to taste
- 1/2 cup cooked brown rice or quinoa (optional)
- 1/2 cup shredded cabbage
- 1/4 cup diced tomatoes
- 1/4 cup diced avocado
- 1/4 cup chopped fresh cilantro
- Juice of 1 lime

DIETARY INFO
Calories 280 | Carbs 12g
Fat 15g | protein 23g
Fiber 4g

DIRECTIONS

1. Preheat your oven to 375°F (190°C) or prepare a grill for medium-high heat.
2. Brush the fish fillets with olive oil and season with chili powder, cumin, salt, and pepper.
3. If baking, place the fish on a lined baking sheet and bake for 10-12 minutes, or until the fish flakes easily with a fork. If grilling, grill the fish for about 3-5 minutes per side, depending on thickness.
4. While the fish is cooking, prepare your bowl base. If using, place cooked brown rice or quinoa in a bowl.
5. Top the grains with shredded cabbage, diced tomatoes, and diced avocado.
6. Once the fish is cooked, flake it with a fork and place it on top of the prepared vegetables.
7. Squeeze fresh lime juice over the bowl and sprinkle with chopped cilantro.
8. Serve immediately, garnished with lime wedges and additional cilantro if desired.

Mushroom Pork Chops

SERVINGS 1   **PREP. TIME** 10 min   **COOKING TIME** 20 min   **DIFFICULTY** Easy

DESCRIPTION

This Mushroom Pork Chops recipe combines simple, wholesome ingredients into a flavorful meal that's easy to prepare and perfectly suited for a healthy eating plan.

INGREDIENTS

- 1 lean pork chop (approximately 150g)
- Salt and pepper to taste
- 1/2 tablespoon olive oil
- 1/2 cup sliced mushrooms
- 1 clove garlic, minced
- 1/2 cup low sodium chicken broth
- 1 tablespoon low-fat sour cream or Greek yogurt
- 1 teaspoon fresh thyme (or 1/2 teaspoon dried thyme)

DIETARY INFO

Calories	250	Carbs	4g
Fat	12g	protein	26g
Fiber	1g		

DIRECTIONS

1. Season the pork chop with salt and pepper on both sides.
2. In a skillet over medium heat, warm the olive oil. Add the pork chop and cook for about 4-5 minutes on each side, or until browned and cooked through to an internal temperature of 145°F (63°C). Remove the pork chop from the skillet and set aside to rest.
3. Place the chopped garlic and sliced mushrooms in the same skillet. Sauté for about 2-3 minutes, until the mushrooms are tender and golden.
4. Pour in the chicken broth and bring to a simmer, scraping any browned bits off the bottom of the skillet.
5. Stir in the sour cream or Greek yogurt and thyme. Cook for another 2-3 minutes, until the sauce is creamy and slightly thickened. Add more salt and pepper to taste.
6. Return the pork chop to the skillet, spooning the mushroom sauce over the top to reheat the meat for about 1-2 minutes.
7. Serve the pork chop hot, garnished with chopped parsley if using.

Chicken Quesadillas

SERVINGS
1

PREP. TIME
15 min

COOKING TIME
10 min

DIFFICULTY
Easy

DESCRIPTION

Chicken Quesadillas are a delightful blend of juicy, seasoned chicken, melted cheese, and a crisp tortilla.

INGREDIENTS

- 1 large whole wheat tortilla
- 150g cooked chicken breast, shredded
- 1/4 cup low-fat cheese, shredded (such as mozzarella or cheddar)
- 1/2 bell pepper, thinly sliced
- 1/2 onion, thinly sliced
- 1 garlic clove, minced
- 1/2 teaspoon chili powder
- 1/2 teaspoon cumin
- Non-stick cooking spray
- Salt and pepper to taste

DIRECTIONS

1. Preheat a skillet over medium heat and spray with non-stick cooking spray.
2. Sauté the bell pepper, onion, and garlic in the skillet until softened, about 3-5 minutes. Season with chili powder, cumin, salt, and pepper.
3. Add the shredded chicken to the skillet and stir to combine with the vegetables. Cook for an additional 2 minutes to heat the chicken through. Remove from heat.
4. Place the whole-wheat tortilla in a neat, level layer. On one half of the tortilla, evenly spread the chicken and vegetable mixture. Top with a scattering of the shredded cheese.
5. Fold the other half of the tortilla over to cover the fillings, forming a half-moon shape.
6. Wipe the skillet clean, then return it to medium heat. Carefully place the filled tortilla in the skillet. Cook for about 2-3 minutes on each side or until the tortilla is golden brown and the cheese has melted.
7. Remove from the skillet and cut into wedges. Serve hot, accompanied by salsa or Greek yogurt if desired.

DIETARY INFO

Calories	300	Carbs	25g
Fat	9g	protein	28g
Fiber	4g		

Chickpea and Feta Salad

SERVINGS 1 | **PREP. TIME** 10 min | **COOKING TIME** 0 min | **DIFFICULTY** Easy

DESCRIPTION

Chickpea and Feta Salad is a vibrant, nutrient-rich dish that combines the creamy texture of feta cheese with the hearty feel of chickpeas, all tossed in a light and flavorful dressing.

INGREDIENTS

- 1 cup canned chickpeas, rinsed and drained
- 1/4 cup crumbled feta cheese (low-fat)
- 1/2 cucumber, diced
- 1/2 red bell pepper, diced
- 1/4 red onion, thinly sliced
- 10 cherry tomatoes, halved
- 2 tablespoons chopped fresh parsley
- Juice of 1 lemon
- 1 tablespoon olive oil
- Salt and pepper to taste

DIRECTIONS

1. In a large bowl, combine the rinsed chickpeas, diced cucumber, diced red bell pepper, sliced red onion, and halved cherry tomatoes.
2. Add the crumbled feta cheese and chopped parsley to the bowl.
3. In a small bowl or jar, whisk together the lemon juice, olive oil, salt, pepper, and optional dried herbs (oregano or mint) to create the dressing.
4. Pour the dressing over the salad ingredients and toss gently to coat everything evenly.
5. Taste and, if needed, adjust the seasoning.
6. Serve the salad immediately, or let it chill in the refrigerator for 30 minutes to allow the flavors to meld together.

DIETARY INFO

Calories	350		Carbs	35g
Fat	18g		protein	15g
Fiber	10g			

Baked Garlic Lemon Salmon

SERVINGS
1

PREP. TIME
10 min

COOKING TIME
20 min

DIFFICULTY
Easy

DESCRIPTION

Baked Garlic Lemon Salmon is an excellent source of high-quality protein and omega-3 fatty acids, making it a heart-healthy option.

INGREDIENTS

- 1 salmon fillet (approximately 150g)
- 2 cloves garlic, minced
- Juice of 1 lemon
- 1 tablespoon olive oil
- Salt and pepper to taste
- Lemon slices for garnish
- Fresh parsley, chopped for garnish

DIRECTIONS

1. Preheat your oven to 375°F (190°C).
2. Place the salmon fillet in a baking dish lined with parchment paper or lightly greased with cooking spray.
3. In a small bowl, mix together the minced garlic, lemon juice, and olive oil.
4. Season the salmon fillet with salt and pepper.
5. Pour the garlic lemon mixture over the salmon, ensuring it is evenly coated.
6. Place a few lemon slices on top of the salmon for added flavor and presentation.
7. Bake for 15 to 20 minutes in a preheated oven, or until the salmon is thoroughly cooked and flake readily with a fork.
8. Remove from the oven and garnish with chopped fresh parsley. Serve immediately.

DIETARY INFO

Calories	300	Carbs	3g
Fat	20g	protein	23g
Fiber	0g		

Baked Buffalo Chicken Taquitos

SERVINGS 1 **PREP. TIME** 15 min **COOKING TIME** 20 min **DIFFICULTY** Easy

DESCRIPTION

Baked Buffalo Chicken Taquitos are a delightful twist on traditional taquitos, combining the fiery zest of buffalo chicken with the crispy texture of baked tortillas.

INGREDIENTS

- 1 large chicken breast (approximately 150g), cooked and shredded
- 1/4 cup low-fat cream cheese, softened
- 2 tablespoons buffalo sauce (adjust based on spice preference)
- 1/2 cup shredded low-fat mozzarella cheese
- 4 small whole wheat tortillas
- Non-stick cooking spray

DIRECTIONS

1. Preheat your oven to 400°F (200°C). Line a baking sheet with parchment paper and lightly spray it with non-stick cooking spray.
2. In a mixing bowl, combine the shredded chicken, softened cream cheese, buffalo sauce, and mozzarella cheese. Blend until all components are thoroughly combined.
3. Spoon an even amount of the chicken mixture down the center of each tortilla. Roll the tortillas tightly around the filling to form the taquitos.
4. Transfer the tacos to the baking sheet that has been prepared, seam side down. Lightly spray the tops with non-stick cooking spray to help them brown.
5. Bake in the preheated oven for 15-20 minutes, or until the taquitos are crispy and golden brown.
6. Remove from the oven and let cool for a few minutes. Optionally, garnish with chopped green onions.
7. Serve warm with low-fat Greek yogurt or light sour cream for dipping if desired.

DIETARY INFO

Calories	350	Carbs	28g
Fat	10g	protein	32g
Fiber	4g		

0 Point Weight Loss Cookbook for Beginners

Balsamic Vinegar Chicken

SERVINGS 1 | **PREP. TIME** 10 min | **COOKING TIME** 20 min | **DIFFICULTY** Easy

DESCRIPTION
Balsamic Vinegar Chicken is a flavorful and aromatic dish that combines the rich, tangy taste of balsamic vinegar with tender chicken, making it a perfect choice for a healthy meal.

INGREDIENTS

- 1 chicken breast (approximately 150g)
- 2 tablespoons balsamic vinegar
- 1 tablespoon olive oil
- 1 clove garlic, minced
- 1/2 teaspoon dried rosemary
- 1/2 teaspoon dried thyme
- Salt and pepper to taste
- 1/2 cup cherry tomatoes, halved
- Fresh basil leaves, for garnish

DIRECTIONS

1. In a small bowl, whisk together the balsamic vinegar, olive oil, minced garlic, rosemary, thyme, salt, and pepper.
2. Place the chicken breast in a shallow dish or a resealable plastic bag. Pour the balsamic vinegar mixture over the chicken, making sure it is well coated. Let it marinate in the refrigerator for at least 30 minutes, or up to 2 hours for more flavor.
3. Preheat the oven to 375°F (190°C).
4. Transfer the marinated chicken along with the marinade into a baking dish. Scatter the halved cherry tomatoes around the chicken.
5. Bake in the preheated oven for 20 minutes, or until the chicken is cooked through and reaches an internal temperature of 165°F (74°C).
6. Remove from the oven and let rest for a few minutes.
7. Serve the chicken sliced, topped with the roasted cherry tomatoes and fresh basil leaves.

DIETARY INFO

Calories	290	Carbs	8g
Fat	15g	protein	26g
Fiber	1g		

Southwest Chicken Salad

SERVINGS 1 | **PREP. TIME** 15 min | **COOKING TIME** 0 min | **DIFFICULTY** Easy

DESCRIPTION

Southwest Chicken Salad is a vibrant and flavorful dish that combines spicy grilled chicken with a mix of colorful vegetables and a zesty lime dressing.

INGREDIENTS

- 150g chicken breast, grilled and sliced
- 1/2 cup canned black beans, rinsed and drained
- 1/2 cup corn kernels (fresh, frozen, or canned and drained)
- 1/2 red bell pepper, diced
- 1/4 cup chopped red onion
- 1/2 avocado, diced
- 1/2 cup cherry tomatoes, halved
- 1/4 cup chopped fresh cilantro
- Juice of 1 lime
- 1 teaspoon olive oil
- 1/2 teaspoon chili powder
- 1/2 teaspoon cumin
- Salt and pepper to taste

DIRECTIONS

1. In a large mixing bowl, combine the grilled and sliced chicken, black beans, corn, red bell pepper, red onion, avocado, and cherry tomatoes.
2. In a small bowl, whisk together the lime juice, olive oil, chili powder, cumin, salt, pepper, and optional cayenne pepper to create the dressing.
3. Drizzle the large bowl of salad components with the dressing. Toss gently to coat everything evenly with the dressing.
4. Sprinkle the chopped cilantro over the salad and toss lightly once more.
5. Serve the salad immediately, or chill in the refrigerator for about 30 minutes before serving to allow the flavors to meld together.

DIETARY INFO

Calories	320		Carbs	28g
Fat	12g		protein	28g
Fiber	8g			

0 Point Weight Loss Cookbook for Beginners

CHAPTER 4

SNACKS

Protein Bistro Boxes

SERVINGS 1 | **PREP. TIME** 10 min | **COOKING TIME** 10 min | **DIFFICULTY** Easy

DESCRIPTION
These bistro-style meal prep snack boxes are packed with a variety of wholesome snacks, perfect for fueling your day whether it's breakfast, lunch, or a healthy snack. With a balance of protein, fruits, and veggies, they'll keep you satisfied and energized!

INGREDIENTS

- 1 packet of Hidden Valley Greek Yogurt Dips Mix
- 1 1/2 cups of plain fat-free Greek yogurt
- 4 hard-boiled eggs
- Chicken breast from a rotisserie chicken, skin removed
- One pint of dried and washed grape tomatoes
- Young carrots, cleaned, then wiped dry
- Sliced, dried, and lightly dusted with lemon juice apples
- Fresh grapes that have been dried and washed
- Salt and freshly ground pepper

DIRECTIONS

1. In a small bowl, mix the Hidden Valley Greek Yogurt Dips mix with the fat-free Greek yogurt.
2. Transfer ranch dip into portion cups, place portion cup lids on top, and save. Any leftover ranch dip can be refrigerated for future use.
3. Assemble the bistro box as shown in the picture, placing each ingredient in its own section.
4. Sprinkle the chicken and hard-boiled eggs with a pinch of kosher salt and freshly ground pepper.
5. Keep the assembled box refrigerated and consume within three days.

DIETARY INFO

Calories	99		Carbs	5g
Fat	6g		protein	7g
Fiber	1g			

0 Point Weight Loss Cookbook for Beginners

White Popcorn Kernels

SERVINGS: 1
PREP. TIME: 10 min
COOKING TIME: 10 min
DIFFICULTY: Easy

DESCRIPTION

With self-popped kernels scoring zero points, you can explore a world of seasoning possibilities, from sweet to savory or a tantalizing blend of both!

INGREDIENTS

- 3 tbsp popcorn kernels

DIRECTIONS

1. Place a single serving of popcorn kernels into the silicone microwave popper.
2. Securely cover with the lid.
3. Microwave for approximately 2 minutes, adjusting according to your microwave's power.
4. Spritz with butter substitute before seasoning.
5. Add your preferred seasoning to customize your popcorn flavor.

DIETARY INFO

Calories	165	Carbs	33g
Fat	2g	protein	8g
Fiber	6g		

0 Point Weight Loss Cookbook for Beginners

Roasted Garbanzo Beans

SERVINGS 1 | **PREP. TIME** 5 min | **COOKING TIME** 30 min | **DIFFICULTY** Easy

DESCRIPTION
This recipe offers a high-protein, high-fiber option that's perfect for snacking or adding a tasty crunch to salads.

INGREDIENTS

- 1 cup canned garbanzo beans (chickpeas), rinsed and drained
- 1 tablespoon olive oil
- 1/2 teaspoon chili powder
- 1/2 teaspoon cumin
- 1/4 teaspoon garlic powder
- 1/4 teaspoon onion powder
- Salt and pepper to taste

DIETARY INFO
- Calories 270
- Fat 21g
- Fiber 8g
- Carbs 30g
- protein 10g

DIRECTIONS

1. Preheat your oven to 400°F (200°C).
2. Pat the garbanzo beans dry with paper towels to remove as much moisture as possible. This step is crucial for achieving maximum crispiness.
3. In a bowl, toss the dried garbanzo beans with olive oil, chili powder, cumin, garlic powder, onion powder, salt, and pepper until evenly coated.
4. Spread the seasoned garbanzo beans in a single layer on a baking sheet lined with parchment paper.
5. Roast in the preheated oven for 25-30 minutes, stirring halfway through, until the beans are golden and crispy.
6. Remove from the oven and let cool on the baking sheet for a few minutes to further crisp up.
7. Serve warm as a snack or use as a topping for salads or soups.

Zero Point Banana Soufflé

SERVINGS 1 | **PREP. TIME** 3 min | **COOKING TIME** 5 min | **DIFFICULTY** Easy

DESCRIPTION

This delightful banana soufflé recipe is perfect for a quick breakfast, a nutritious snack. Packed with natural proteins and simple, wholesome ingredients, it's both satisfying and health-conscious.

INGREDIENTS

- 2 bananas
- 2 eggs

DIRECTIONS

1. Use a fork to thoroughly mash the bananas in a mixing bowl.
2. Crack the eggs into the bowl with the mashed bananas.
3. Stir the mixture vigorously until well combined.
4. Pour the mixture into a microwave-safe dish and cook on high for 3 minutes. After cooking, check the consistency; if it needs more firmness, microwave for an additional minute.
5. Optionally, garnish with a dash of cinnamon before serving for added flavor.

DIETARY INFO

Calories	336		Carbs	55g
Fat	9g		protein	14g
Fiber	6g			

0 Point Weight Loss Cookbook for Beginners

Instant Pot Premier Protein Yogurt

SERVINGS 1   **PREP. TIME** 10 min   **COOKING TIME** 8 hour   **DIFFICULTY** Easy

DESCRIPTION
This particular recipe uses Premier Protein shake to boost the protein content, making it an ideal choice for a zero-point weight loss diet. It's perfect for breakfast, a snack, or as a base in smoothies recipes.

INGREDIENTS

- 1 quart (4 cups) non-fat plain Greek yogurt
- 1 cup Premier Protein shake (vanilla flavor recommended)
- 2 tablespoons plain non-fat yogurt (with live cultures) to use as a starter

DIRECTIONS

1. If your Instant Pot has a yogurt setting, ensure the inner pot is clean and dry before adding the ingredients.
2. In a mixing bowl, combine the Greek yogurt, Premier Protein shake, and the two tablespoons of plain yogurt. Mix thoroughly until completely smooth.
3. Pour the mixture into the Instant Pot.
4. Close the lid (vent closed) and select the 'Yogurt' setting. Adjust the time to 8 hours, allowing the Instant Pot to incubate the yogurt.
5. After 8 hours, the yogurt will have thickened and cultured. Open the lid and stir the yogurt to ensure uniform consistency.
6. Chill the yogurt after transferring it to sealed jars. The yogurt will set further and thicken up once cooled.
7. Serve chilled. Add fresh fruits, nuts, or honey for flavoring if desired, but remember to account for any additional points these might add.

DIETARY INFO

Calories	90	Carbs	7g
Fat	0g	protein	15g
Fiber	0g		

Sunshine Salad

SERVINGS	PREP. TIME	COOKING TIME	DIFFICULTY
1	10 min	0 min	Easy

DESCRIPTION

Sunshine Salad is a vibrant, refreshing dish perfect for any season. Bursting with a mix of sweet and citrus flavors, this salad combines fruits and vegetables for a delightful side or main dish.

INGREDIENTS

- 1/2 cup chopped fresh pineapple
- 1/2 orange, peeled and sectioned
- 1/4 cup sliced strawberries
- 1/4 cup blueberries
- 1/4 avocado, diced
- 2 tablespoons sliced almonds (optional,)
- Juice of 1/2 lemon
- 1 tablespoon chopped fresh mint
- Salt and pepper to taste

DIRECTIONS

1. In a large mixing bowl, combine the chopped pineapple, orange sections, sliced strawberries, and blueberries.
2. Add the diced avocado to the bowl.
3. Squeeze the lemon juice over the fruits, and gently toss everything together to mix. Be careful not to crush the fruits.
4. Sprinkle the chopped fresh mint over the salad for a burst of freshness.
5. If using, scatter the sliced almonds on top for a crunchy texture.
6. Season lightly with salt and pepper to balance the sweetness.
7. Serve immediately to enjoy the freshest flavors, or refrigerate for up to an hour to allow the flavors to meld together more.

DIETARY INFO

Calories	150		Carbs	25g
Fat	5g		protein	2g
Fiber	4g			

Red Lentil Crepes

SERVINGS 1 | **PREP. TIME** 15 min | **COOKING TIME** 20 min | **DIFFICULTY** Easy

DESCRIPTION
Red Lentil Crepes are a nutritious, gluten-free alternative to traditional crepes, made entirely from red lentils for a high-protein, high-fiber meal.

INGREDIENTS

- 1 cup red lentils, soaked for 4 hours or overnight
- 1 cup water
- 1/2 teaspoon salt
- 1/2 teaspoon cumin (optional, for savory crepes)
- Non-stick cooking spray or a small amount of olive oil for cooking

DIETARY INFO
Calories	240	Carbs	40g
Fat	1g	protein	18g
Fiber	8g		

DIRECTIONS

1. Drain the soaked red lentils and rinse them under cold water until the water runs clear.
2. In a blender, combine the soaked red lentils, water, salt, and cumin (if making savory crepes). Blend until the mixture is smooth and has the consistency of a thin batter.
3. Turn on a medium heat source for a nonstick skillet. Lightly grease the pan with non-stick cooking spray or a small amount of olive oil.
4. Pour a small amount of the lentil batter into the center of the skillet. Tilt the pan in a circular motion to spread the batter thinly across the surface.
5. Cook for about 2-3 minutes, or until the edges of the crepe start to lift from the pan and the bottom is lightly golden. Carefully flip the crepe with a spatula and cook for an additional 1-2 minutes on the other side.
6. Take out the crepe and put it onto a plate from the griddle. Repeat with the remaining batter, adjusting the pan's heat as needed to prevent burning.
7. Serve the crepes warm. They can be filled with a variety of fillings such as fresh vegetables and herbs, low-fat cheese, or even fruit and yogurt for a sweet version.

0 Point Weight Loss Cookbook for Beginners

Hashbrown Potatoes

SERVINGS	**PREP. TIME**	**COOKING TIME**	**DIFFICULTY**
1	15 min	25 min	Easy

DESCRIPTION

This recipe uses a simple, health-conscious method to prepare crispy, golden hashbrowns without the need for excessive oil, making them a perfect fit for a nutritious meal plan.

INGREDIENTS

- 2 medium potatoes, peeled
- Salt and pepper to taste
- Non-stick cooking spray

DIRECTIONS

1. Grate the peeled potatoes using the large holes of a box grater.
2. Transfer the grated potatoes to a clean cloth or paper towel and squeeze out as much moisture as possible. This step is crucial for achieving crispy hashbrowns.
3. Heat a non-stick skillet over medium-high heat and coat with non-stick cooking spray.
4. Spread the grated potatoes evenly in the skillet, pressing them down lightly with a spatula. Season with salt and pepper.
5. Cook for about 10-12 minutes, or until the bottom is golden brown and crispy. Carefully flip the hashbrown using a large spatula (you may divide it into sections if easier) and cook the other side for another 10-12 minutes until crispy.
6. Take out of the skillet and serve right away. Optional: Garnish with chopped fresh herbs like parsley or chives for added flavor.

DIETARY INFO

Calories	150		Carbs	34g
Fat	0g		protein	4g
Fiber	4g			

No Bake Brownies Without Added Sugar

SERVINGS 1 | **PREP. TIME** 15 min | **COOKING TIME** 1 hour | **DIFFICULTY** Easy

DESCRIPTION

These No Bake Brownies are a delightful treat that doesn't require any baking or added sugars, making them perfect for anyone following a zero-point weight loss plan.

INGREDIENTS

- 1 cup pitted dates, soaked in warm water for 10 minutes to soften
- 1/2 cup raw unsweetened cocoa powder
- 1 cup raw walnuts
- 1 teaspoon vanilla extract
- A pinch of salt
- Optional: 1/4 cup unsweetened shredded coconut or chopped nuts for topping

DIRECTIONS

1. Drain the soaked dates and place them in a food processor along with the walnuts, cocoa powder, vanilla extract, and a pinch of salt.
2. Process until the mixture is finely ground and starts to clump together. If the mixture seems too dry, add a tablespoon of water at a time until it reaches a sticky, dough-like consistency.
3. Line a small baking dish or tray with parchment paper.
4. Transfer the brownie mixture to the lined dish. Press firmly into an even layer using the back of a spoon or your hands.
5. If using, sprinkle the top with shredded coconut or chopped nuts and press lightly to adhere.
6. To set, refrigerate for a minimum of one hour. This facilitates slicing the brownies.
7. When set, cut into squares or any shapes that you like, then serve.

DIETARY INFO

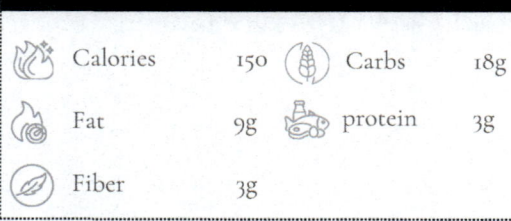

Calories	150	Carbs	18g
Fat	9g	protein	3g
Fiber	3g		

White Chicken Chili

SERVINGS: 1
PREP. TIME: 15 min
COOKING TIME: 25 min
DIFFICULTY: Easy

DESCRIPTION

It's packed with lean chicken, white beans, and plenty of spices, offering a hearty, comforting meal that fits perfectly into a zero-point weight loss plan when prepared with mindful ingredient choices.

INGREDIENTS

- 150g chicken breast, cooked and shredded
- 1/2 cup chopped onions
- 2 cloves garlic, minced
- 1 cup low-sodium chicken broth
- 1 can (about 1.5 cups) white beans (such as cannellini or Great Northern), rinsed and drained
- 1/2 teaspoon chili powder
- 1/2 teaspoon cumin
- 1/4 teaspoon oregano
- 1/4 teaspoon cayenne pepper (optional, adjust to taste)
- Salt and pepper to taste
- 1/4 cup chopped cilantro for garnish
- 1/2 lime, juiced

DIRECTIONS

1. Turn up the heat to medium in a big saucepan. Add a splash of water or a light spray of cooking oil, then sauté the onions and garlic until translucent, about 5 minutes.
2. Stir in the chili powder, cumin, oregano, and cayenne pepper. Cook until the spices become fragrant, about one more minute.
3. Add the shredded chicken, white beans, and chicken broth to the pot. Stir to combine.
4. Bring the mixture to a boil, then reduce the heat to low and simmer for 15-20 minutes to allow the flavors to meld together.
5. To taste, add salt and pepper for seasoning. Just before serving, stir in the lime juice and garnish with chopped cilantro.
6. Serve hot. For an additional zero-point boost, top with sliced jalapeños or a dollop of fat-free Greek yogurt.

DIETARY INFO

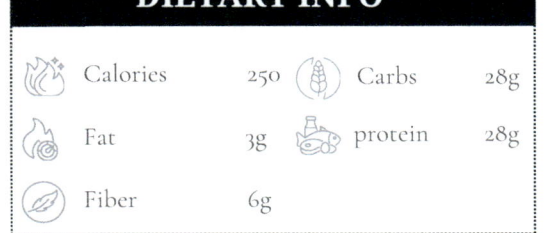

- Calories: 250
- Fat: 3g
- Fiber: 6g
- Carbs: 28g
- protein: 28g

Easy Cucumber Chips

SERVINGS 1 | **PREP. TIME** 10 min | **COOKING TIME** 3 hour | **DIFFICULTY** Easy

DESCRIPTION

Easy Cucumber Chips are a light, crispy snack made with just a few simple ingredients, these chips offer a healthy alternative to traditional snacks, with the added benefit of being low in calories.

INGREDIENTS

- 2 large cucumbers
- Salt to taste
- Optional: vinegar, chili powder, or dried dill for flavoring

DIRECTIONS

1. Preheat your oven to 200°F (93°C) if using an oven to dehydrate, or prepare your dehydrator.
2. Thinly slice the cucumbers using a mandoline slicer for uniform thickness.
3. Lay out the cucumber slices on paper towels and lightly salt them. Allow them to sit for ten to fifteen minutes in order to extract extra moisture. With another paper towel, pat them dry.
4. If using, sprinkle your choice of additional seasonings such as chili powder or dried dill.
5. Arrange the cucumber slices in a single layer on a baking sheet lined with parchment paper, if using an oven, or on dehydrator trays.
6. Dehydrate in the oven or dehydrator. If using an oven, bake for approximately 3-4 hours, flipping the slices every hour to ensure even drying. If using a dehydrator, follow the manufacturer's instructions, usually set at 135°F for about 4-5 hours.
7. The cucumber chips are done when they are crispy and no longer moist.
8. Allow the chips to cool completely before storing them in an airtight container to maintain their crispness.

DIETARY INFO

Calories	50	Carbs	12g
Fat	0g	protein	2g
Fiber	2g		

Pickle Wraps

SERVINGS: 1
PREP. TIME: 10 min
COOKING TIME: 0 min
DIFFICULTY: Easy

DESCRIPTION

Pickle wraps are a simple, delicious snack that combines the tangy flavor of pickles with the creamy texture of cheese and the savory taste of deli meats, all wrapped up in a convenient package.

INGREDIENTS

- 2 large dill pickles
- 4 slices of deli turkey breast (look for low-sodium, zero-point options if possible)
- 2 tablespoons fat-free cream cheese
- Optional: sprinkle of dried herbs or black pepper for extra flavor

DIRECTIONS

1. Lay out the turkey breast slices on a clean surface.
2. Spread each slice with about 1/2 tablespoon of fat-free cream cheese. If desired, sprinkle a little dried herbs or black pepper over the cream cheese for added flavor.
3. Place a dill pickle at the edge of each turkey slice.
4. Carefully roll the turkey around the pickle. Make sure the wrap is tight so it holds together well.
5. Once all the pickles are wrapped, you can either cut them into rounds to serve as appetizers or keep them whole as a snack.
6. Serve immediately, or chill in the refrigerator before serving for a firmer texture.

DIETARY INFO

Calories	100		Carbs	4g
Fat	1g		protein	15g
Fiber	1g			

Frozen Grapes

SERVINGS 1 | **PREP. TIME** 5 min | **COOKING TIME** 0 min | **DIFFICULTY** Easy

DESCRIPTION

Frozen grapes are a simple, sweet treat that's refreshing and perfect for snacking without any guilt.

INGREDIENTS

- 1 cup fresh grapes

DIRECTIONS

1. Wash the grapes thoroughly.
2. Pat them dry and spread them out on a baking sheet lined with parchment paper.
3. Freeze for 2-3 hours until solid.
4. Transfer to a freezer bag or container for longer storage.

DIETARY INFO

Calories	0	Carbs	27g
Fat	0g	protein	1g
Fiber	1g		

Cabbage Soup

SERVINGS	PREP. TIME	COOKING TIME	DIFFICULTY
1	10 min	25 min	Easy

DESCRIPTION

Cabbage soup is a hearty, filling dish that's loaded with nutrients and perfect for filling you up without adding points to your diet.

INGREDIENTS

- 2 cups chopped cabbage
- 1 cup diced onion
- 1/2 cup diced carrots
- 1/2 cup diced green bell pepper
- 2 minced garlic cloves
- 3 cups vegetable broth (zero sodium if available)
- 1 tsp paprika
- Salt and pepper to taste

DIRECTIONS

1. In a large pot, spray with non-stick cooking spray. Add onion, garlic, carrots, and green pepper. Sauté until soft.
2. Add the cabbage, vegetable broth, and paprika.
3. Bring to a boil, then reduce heat and simmer for 20 minutes.
4. To taste, add salt and pepper for seasoning. Warm up the food.

DIETARY INFO

Calories	0		Carbs	20g
Fat	0g		protein	3g
Fiber	6g			

Tofu Chips

SERVINGS 1 | **PREP. TIME** 10 min | **COOKING TIME** 20 min | **DIFFICULTY** Easy

DESCRIPTION
Tofu chips are a crunchy, savory snack that's low in calories and high in protein, perfect for satisfying your crunch cravings without breaking your diet.

INGREDIENTS

- 1 block firm tofu, pressed and sliced into thin pieces
- Salt and pepper to taste
- Optional: chili powder or other seasoning

DIRECTIONS

1. Set your oven to 375°F (190°C).
2. Arrange tofu slices on a baking sheet lined with parchment paper.
3. Season with salt, pepper, and optional spices.
4. Bake for 20 minutes, flipping halfway through until crispy.
5. Let cool before serving.

DIETARY INFO

Calories	0		Carbs	2g
Fat	4g		protein	8g
Fiber	1g			

Mexican Zero Point Soup

SERVINGS
1

PREP. TIME
10 min

COOKING TIME
20 min

DIFFICULTY
Easy

DESCRIPTION

This vibrant Mexican Zero Point Soup is brimming with flavors from fresh vegetables and herbs, making it a perfect addition to any weight loss diet without costing you any points.

INGREDIENTS

- 1 cup chopped tomatoes
- 1/2 cup diced onions
- 1 minced garlic clove
- 1 chopped bell pepper
- 1/2 cup sliced carrots
- 1/2 cup chopped celery
- 1 cup vegetable broth
- 1 tsp cumin
- 1 tsp chili powder
- 1/2 cup chopped cilantro
- Salt and pepper to taste

DIRECTIONS

1. In a large pot, spray some zero-calorie cooking spray and sauté onions and garlic until soft.
2. Add bell pepper, carrots, and celery. Cook for about 5 minutes.
3. Stir in tomatoes, vegetable broth, cumin, and chili powder. Bring to a boil.
4. Reduce heat and simmer for 15 minutes until vegetables are tender.
5. Season with salt and pepper. Before serving, garnish with cilantro.

DIETARY INFO

Calories	0		Carbs	20g
Fat	0g		protein	3g
Fiber	5g			

0 Point Weight Loss Cookbook for Beginners

Baked Sweet Potato Chips

SERVINGS: 1
PREP. TIME: 10 min
COOKING TIME: 20 min
DIFFICULTY: Easy

DESCRIPTION

Baked Sweet Potato Chips are light, crispy, and flavored with a hint of spices, making them a perfect snack for anyone following a zero-point weight loss plan.

INGREDIENTS

- 1 large sweet potato, thinly sliced (use a mandoline slicer for best results)
- 1 tablespoon olive oil
- 1/2 teaspoon paprika
- Salt to taste (optional)

DIRECTIONS

1. Set the oven temperature to 375°F, or 190°C. Line a baking sheet with parchment paper.
2. Wash the sweet potato thoroughly and slice it very thinly, aiming for even thickness to ensure even cooking.
3. In a large bowl, toss the sweet potato slices with olive oil, paprika, and a light sprinkle of salt if desired.
4. Arrange the slices in a single layer on the prepared baking sheet, making sure they do not overlap.
5. Bake in the preheated oven for 10-12 minutes, then flip the slices and continue baking for another 10-13 minutes. Watch closely during the last few minutes to prevent burning, as oven temperatures may vary.
6. Remove the chips from the oven when they are crisp and slightly browned. They will continue to crisp up as they cool.
7. Serve the sweet potato chips while they are fresh and crispy.

DIETARY INFO

- Calories: 200
- Carbs: 31g
- Fat: 7g
- protein: 2g
- Fiber: 5g

Two Ingredient Pumpkin Muffins

SERVINGS
1

PREP. TIME
5 min

COOKING TIME
20 min

DIFFICULTY
Easy

DESCRIPTION

Two Ingredient Pumpkin Muffins are incredibly easy to make and deliciously satisfying, using just two simple ingredients for a delightful autumnal treat.

INGREDIENTS

- 1 can (15 oz) pumpkin puree
- 1 box spice cake mix

DIRECTIONS

1. Preheat your oven to 350°F (175°C).
2. In a bowl, mix the pumpkin puree and spice cake mix until well combined.
3. Scoop the batter into a muffin tin lined with paper liners.
4. Bake for 20 minutes or until a toothpick comes out clean.
5. Let cool before serving.

DIETARY INFO

Calories	0		Carbs	24g
Fat	0g		protein	2g
Fiber	3g			

CHAPTER 5

VEGETARIAN

Broccoli & Cheddar Quiche

SERVINGS
1

PREP. TIME
15 min

COOKING TIME
35 min

DIFFICULTY
Easy

DESCRIPTION

This Broccoli & Cheddar Quiche combines the goodness of broccoli with creamy cheddar in a light and fluffy egg base, perfect for a hearty breakfast or a light dinner.

INGREDIENTS

- 1 cup chopped broccoli (steamed)
- 1/2 cup shredded fat-free cheddar cheese
- 1 cup egg whites
- 1/2 cup diced onions
- Salt and pepper to taste
- Non-stick cooking spray

DIRECTIONS

1. Turn the oven down to 350°F/175°C.
2. Spray a pie dish with non-stick cooking spray.
3. Spread the steamed broccoli and diced onions evenly across the bottom of the dish.
4. Sprinkle shredded cheddar over the vegetables.
5. In a bowl, whisk together the egg whites, salt, and pepper. Pour this mixture over the broccoli and cheese.
6. Bake for 35 minutes or until the center is set and the edges are golden brown.
7. Allow it cool for five minutes, then cut into slices and serve.

DIETARY INFO

Calories	100	Carbs	10g
Fat	1g	protein	15g
Fiber	2g		

Grilled Summer Vegetables

SERVINGS
1

PREP. TIME
10 min

COOKING TIME
15 min

DIFFICULTY
Easy

DESCRIPTION

A colorful medley of summer vegetables, grilled to perfection, enhancing their natural sweetness and flavors, ideal for a healthy side dish.

INGREDIENTS

- 1 zucchini, sliced
- 1 yellow squash, sliced
- 1 bell pepper, sliced
- 1/2 red onion, sliced
- 1 tablespoon olive oil
- Salt and pepper to taste

DIRECTIONS

1. Turn the heat up to medium-high on the grill.
2. Toss the sliced vegetables with olive oil, salt, and pepper in a large bowl.
3. Place vegetables on the grill and cook for about 7-8 minutes on each side, or until tender and charred.
4. If preferred, top hot dish with freshly chopped herbs.

DIETARY INFO

Calories	120	Carbs	15g
Fat	7g	protein	3g
Fiber	5g		

Grilled Cheddar Cheese Sandwiches with Pickles

SERVINGS	PREP. TIME	COOKING TIME	DIFFICULTY
1	5 min	10 min	Easy

DESCRIPTION
A classic grilled cheese sandwich with the tangy twist of pickles, made healthier with fat-free cheddar and whole-grain bread.

INGREDIENTS

- 2 slices whole grain bread
- 1/4 cup shredded fat-free cheddar cheese
- 2-3 slices of pickles
- Non-stick cooking spray

DIRECTIONS

1. Spray a non-stick skillet with cooking spray and heat over medium heat.
2. Assemble the sandwich by placing cheese and pickles between two slices of bread.
3. Grill the sandwich in the skillet, pressing down with a spatula, for about 5 minutes on each side or until the bread is toasted and the cheese is melted.
4. Serve hot.

DIETARY INFO

Calories	180		Carbs	28g
Fat	2g		protein	12g
Fiber	5g			

0 Point Weight Loss Cookbook for Beginners

Tomato Basil Soup

SERVINGS 1 | **PREP. TIME** 10 min | **COOKING TIME** 30 min | **DIFFICULTY** Easy

DESCRIPTION
A light and refreshing tomato basil soup, perfect for any season, featuring the bright flavors of fresh tomatoes and basil.

INGREDIENTS

- 2 cups chopped fresh tomatoes
- 1/4 cup fresh basil leaves
- 1 cup vegetable broth
- 1 minced garlic clove
- Salt and pepper to taste
- 1/2 cup chopped onions

DIRECTIONS

1. In a pot, sauté onions and garlic with a bit of non-stick spray until translucent.
2. Add chopped tomatoes and vegetable broth. Bring to a boil.
3. Reduce heat and simmer for 20 minutes.
4. Add basil, salt, and pepper. Use an immersion blender to puree the soup until smooth.
5. Serve hot, garnished with a few fresh basil leaves.

DIETARY INFO

Calories	90		Carbs	20g
Fat	1g		protein	4g
Fiber	4g			

Easy Fried Rice

SERVINGS 1 | **PREP. TIME** 10 min | **COOKING TIME** 15 min | **DIFFICULTY** Easy

DESCRIPTION

A simple and quick fried rice dish, packed with vegetables and flavors, using zero-point ingredients to keep it light and healthy.

INGREDIENTS

- 1 cup cooked brown rice (cold, preferably day-old)
- 1/2 cup mixed vegetables (carrots, peas, and corn)
- 1/2 cup chopped onions
- 2 egg whites
- 1 tbsp soy sauce (low sodium)
- 1 tsp sesame oil
- Salt and pepper to taste

DIRECTIONS

1. In a large skillet or wok, heat the sesame oil over medium-high heat.
2. Add onions and sauté until they start to soften.
3. Add mixed vegetables and cook until just tender.
4. Push the vegetables to the side of the skillet and add egg whites to the center. Scramble until cooked through.
5. Add rice and soy sauce. Stir everything together and cook until the rice is hot and slightly crispy.
6. Season with salt and pepper. Serve hot.

DIETARY INFO

Calories	320	Carbs	55g
Fat	5g	protein	12g
Fiber	6g		

0 Point Weight Loss Cookbook for Beginners

Zucchini Noodle Caprese

SERVINGS: 1
PREP. TIME: 10 min
COOKING TIME: 0 min
DIFFICULTY: Easy

DESCRIPTION

A refreshing twist on classic Caprese salad, using spiralized zucchini noodles instead of traditional pasta, making it light and zero-point.

INGREDIENTS

- 1 large zucchini, spiralized
- Half a cup of cherry tomatoes
- 1/4 cup fresh mozzarella balls (optional)
- Fresh basil leaves
- Balsamic glaze (optional)
- Salt and pepper to taste

DIRECTIONS

1. Combine spiralized zucchini, cherry tomatoes, and mozzarella balls in a bowl.
2. Tear fresh basil leaves and sprinkle over the top.
3. Drizzle with balsamic glaze if using. Season with salt and pepper.
4. Toss gently and serve fresh.

DIETARY INFO

Calories	100		Carbs	10g
Fat	4g		protein	6g
Fiber	2g			

0 Point Weight Loss Cookbook for Beginners

Super-easy Slow-Cooker Three-Bean Chili

SERVINGS: 1
PREP. TIME: 10 min
COOKING TIME: 6 hour
DIFFICULTY: Easy

DESCRIPTION
This hearty three-bean chili is packed with protein and flavor, slow-cooked to perfection, and absolutely easy to make.

INGREDIENTS
- 1/2 cup black beans, rinsed and drained
- 1/2 cup kidney beans, rinsed and drained
- 1/2 cup pinto beans, rinsed and drained
- 2 cups diced tomatoes
- 1 cup vegetable broth
- 1/2 cup chopped onions
- 1 minced garlic clove
- 1 tsp chili powder
- 1/2 tsp cumin
- Salt and pepper to taste

DIRECTIONS
1. In a slow cooker, combine all ingredients.
2. Cook on low for 6-8 hours or on high for 3-4 hours.
3. Before serving, make any necessary spice adjustments.

DIETARY INFO
- Calories: 300
- Fat: 2g
- Fiber: 15g
- Carbs: 55g
- protein: 18g

Vegetable Soup

SERVINGS	PREP. TIME	COOKING TIME	DIFFICULTY
1	15 min	30 min	Easy

DESCRIPTION

A warm, comforting bowl of vegetable soup packed with a variety of veggies, perfect for any day.

INGREDIENTS

- 1/2 cup chopped carrots
- 1/2 cup diced potatoes
- 1/2 cup chopped celery
- 1/2 cup chopped onions
- 2 cups vegetable broth
- 1 cup diced tomatoes
- 1 tsp dried herbs (thyme, oregano)
- Salt and pepper to taste

DIRECTIONS

1. In a large pot, heat a bit of water or vegetable broth over medium heat. Add onions and garlic and sauté until translucent.
2. Add carrots, celery, and potatoes, cooking for about 5 minutes.
3. Pour in the broth and tomatoes. Bring to a boil.
4. Reduce heat to a simmer and add dried herbs. Cover and cook for about 20 minutes or until vegetables are tender.
5. Season with salt and pepper to taste. Serve hot.

DIETARY INFO

Calories	300	Carbs	55g
Fat	2g	protein	18g
Fiber	15g		

Fresh Vegetable Soup

SERVINGS 1 | **PREP. TIME** 10 min | **COOKING TIME** 20 min | **DIFFICULTY** Easy

DESCRIPTION

This Fresh Vegetable Soup is a light, nourishing dish filled with a variety of vegetables, perfect for a quick lunch or a comforting dinner.

INGREDIENTS

- 1/2 cup chopped carrots
- 1/2 cup diced zucchini
- 1/2 cup chopped celery
- 1/2 cup chopped onions
- 2 cups vegetable broth (zero sodium if available)
- 1 cup chopped tomatoes
- 1 tsp dried basil
- Salt and pepper to taste

DIRECTIONS

1. In a large pot, heat a bit of water or vegetable broth over medium heat. Add onions and garlic and sauté until translucent.
2. Add carrots, celery, zucchini, and tomatoes, cooking for about 5 minutes.
3. Pour in the broth and add dried basil. Bring to a boil.
4. Reduce heat to a simmer and cook for about 15 minutes or until vegetables are tender.
5. Season with salt and pepper to taste. Serve hot.

DIETARY INFO

Calories	120	Carbs	25g
Fat	1g	protein	4g
Fiber	6g		

Roasted Mixed Vegetables

SERVINGS 1 | **PREP. TIME** 10 min | **COOKING TIME** 25 min | **DIFFICULTY** Easy

DESCRIPTION

A simple and delicious side dish, these Roasted Mixed Vegetables are seasoned with herbs and roasted to perfection.

INGREDIENTS

- 1/2 cup chopped carrots
- 1/2 cup sliced bell peppers
- 1/2 cup broccoli florets
- 1/2 cup cauliflower florets
- 1 tablespoon olive oil
- 1 tsp dried thyme
- Salt and pepper to taste

DIRECTIONS

1. Turn the oven up to 425°F (220°C).
2. Toss the vegetables with olive oil, thyme, salt, and pepper in a large bowl.
3. Spread the vegetables on a baking sheet in a single layer.
4. Roast for 25 minutes, stirring halfway through, until vegetables are tender and caramelized.
5. Serve warm.

DIETARY INFO

Calories	150	Carbs	20g
Fat	7g	protein	4g
Fiber	6g		

0 Point Weight Loss Cookbook for Beginners

Cucumber Noodle Salad

SERVINGS	PREP. TIME	COOKING TIME	DIFFICULTY
1	10 min	0 min	Easy

DESCRIPTION
This refreshing Cucumber Noodle Salad is perfect for a light lunch or as a side dish, featuring spiralized cucumber noodles tossed with a vibrant dressing.

INGREDIENTS

- 1 large cucumber, spiralized
- 1/4 cup sliced red onions
- 1/4 cup chopped tomatoes
- 2 tablespoons apple cider vinegar
- 1 tablespoon olive oil
- Salt and pepper to taste
- Fresh herbs for garnish, such parsley or dill

DIRECTIONS

1. In a large bowl, combine the spiralized cucumber, red onions, and tomatoes.
2. In a small bowl, whisk together apple cider vinegar, olive oil, salt, and pepper.
3. Pour the dressing over the cucumber noodles and toss to coat evenly.
4. Before serving, garnish with fresh herbs.. Serve chilled or at room temperature.

DIETARY INFO

Calories	140	Carbs	12g
Fat	10g	protein	2g
Fiber	2g		

0 Point Weight Loss Cookbook for Beginners

Grilled Asparagus with Lemon

SERVINGS 1 | **PREP. TIME** 5 min | **COOKING TIME** 10 min | **DIFFICULTY** Easy

DESCRIPTION

Grilled Asparagus with Lemon is a simple yet flavorful side dish that pairs well with any meal, highlighting the fresh taste of asparagus with a zesty lemon twist.

INGREDIENTS

- 1 bunch asparagus, trimmed
- 1 tablespoon olive oil
- Salt and pepper to taste
- Lemon wedges for serving

DIRECTIONS

1. Turn the heat up to medium-high on the grill.
2. Toss asparagus with olive oil, salt, and pepper.
3. Grill asparagus for about 10 minutes, turning occasionally, until tender and slightly charred.
4. Squeeze lemon over grilled asparagus before serving.

DIETARY INFO

Calories	100	Carbs	8g
Fat	7g	protein	4g
Fiber	2g		

Carrot and Apple Slaw

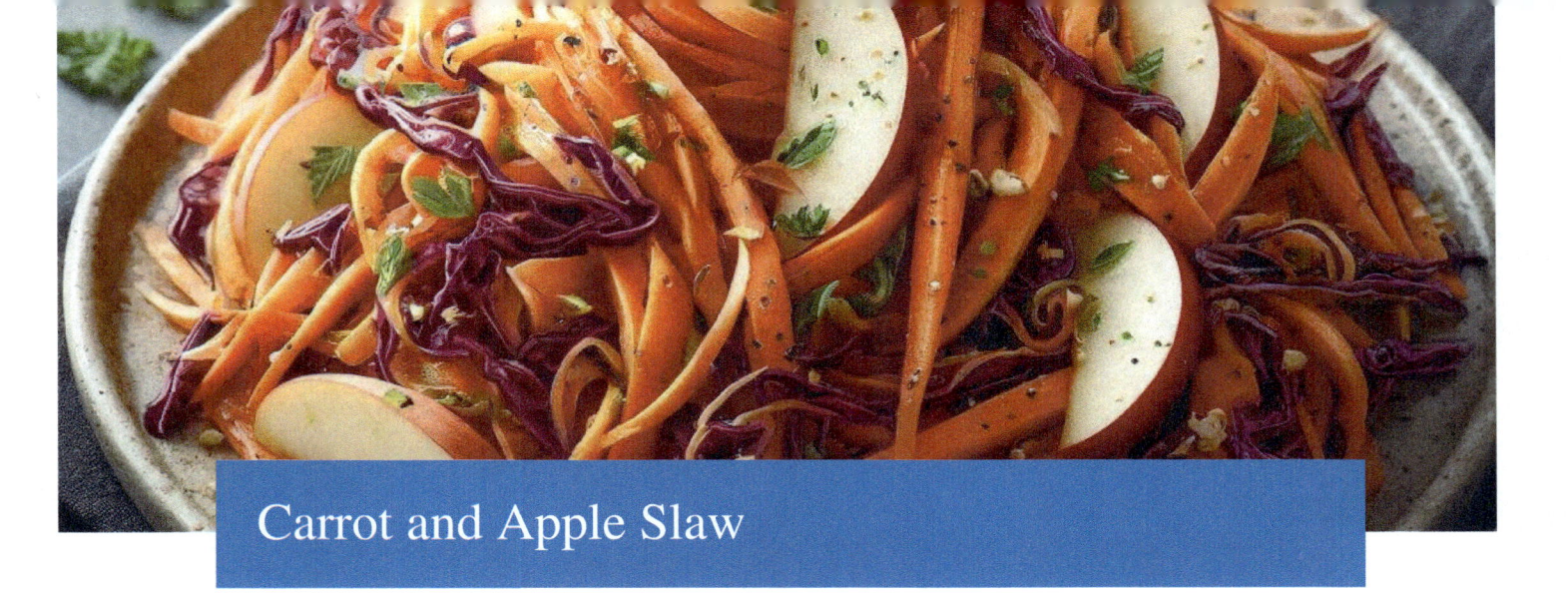

SERVINGS	PREP. TIME	COOKING TIME	DIFFICULTY
1	15 min	0 min	Easy

DESCRIPTION

Carrot and Apple Slaw is a crisp and sweet side dish, perfect for picnics or as a refreshing addition to any meal.

INGREDIENTS

- 1 cup grated carrots
- 1 cup grated apples
- One-fourth cup of apple cider vinegar
- 1 tablespoon honey (optional)
- Salt and pepper to taste

DIRECTIONS

1. In a large bowl, mix together grated carrots and apples.
2. In a small bowl, whisk together apple cider vinegar, honey (if using), salt, and pepper.
3. Pour the dressing over the carrot and apple mixture and toss to combine thoroughly.
4. Chill before serving to allow flavors to meld.

DIETARY INFO

Calories	120	Carbs	30g
Fat	17g	protein	1g
Fiber	5g		

Stir-Fried Bok Choy

SERVINGS 1   **PREP. TIME** 5 min   **COOKING TIME** 5 min   **DIFFICULTY** Easy

DESCRIPTION
Stir-Fried Bok Choy is a quick and healthy dish, featuring the mild, leafy green sautéed with garlic for a flavorful, low-calorie side.

INGREDIENTS
- 2 cups chopped bok choy
- 1 minced garlic clove
- 1 tablespoon soy sauce (low sodium)
- 1 teaspoon sesame oil
- Salt and pepper to taste

DIRECTIONS
1. Heat sesame oil in a large skillet or wok over medium heat.
2. Add garlic and sauté for about 30 seconds until fragrant.
3. Add bok choy and stir-fry for about 3-4 minutes until leaves are wilted and stalks are tender but crisp.
4. Drizzle soy sauce over the bok choy during the last minute of cooking. To taste, add salt and pepper for seasoning. Serve right away.

DIETARY INFO
Calories	60		Carbs	6g
Fat	3g		protein	3g
Fiber	2g			

Mushroom and Spinach Saute

SERVINGS: 1
PREP. TIME: 5 min
COOKING TIME: 10 min
DIFFICULTY: Easy

DESCRIPTION

Mushroom and Spinach Saute is a savory and earthy dish, combining the rich flavors of mushrooms with the freshness of spinach, perfect as a quick side or a light main dish.

INGREDIENTS

- 1 cup sliced mushrooms
- 2 cups spinach leaves
- 1 minced garlic clove
- 1 tablespoon olive oil
- Salt and pepper to taste

DIRECTIONS

1. In a big skillet over medium heat, warm up the olive oil.
2. Add garlic and mushrooms, sautéing until mushrooms are golden, about 5 minutes.
3. Add spinach and cook until wilted, about 3-4 minutes.
4. To taste, add salt and pepper for seasoning. Warm up the food.

DIETARY INFO

- Calories: 90
- Fat: 7g
- Fiber: 2g
- Carbs: 6g
- protein: 5g

CHAPTER 6

DESSERT

Berry and Lime Parfait

SERVINGS 1 **PREP. TIME** 10 min **COOKING TIME** 0 min **DIFFICULTY** Easy

DESCRIPTION
This Berry and Lime Parfait combines the tangy zest of lime with the natural sweetness of berries, layered with light yogurt for a refreshing and healthy dessert or snack.

INGREDIENTS

- 1 cup mixed berries (strawberries, blueberries, raspberries)
- 1 cup fat-free Greek yogurt
- Zest of 1 lime
- 1 tablespoon lime juice
- Optional: sweetener of choice to taste

DIRECTIONS

1. In a small bowl, mix Greek yogurt with lime zest, lime juice, and sweetener if using.
2. In a serving glass, layer half of the berries, followed by half of the yogurt mixture. Repeat the layers.
3. Garnish with a few whole berries and a sprinkle of lime zest on top.
4. Serve immediately or chill in the refrigerator before serving for enhanced flavors.

DIETARY INFO

- Calories: 150
- Fat: 0g
- Fiber: 3g
- Carbs: 20g
- protein: 15g

0 Point Weight Loss Cookbook for Beginners

Chilled Watermelon Soup

SERVINGS 1 | **PREP. TIME** 10 min | **COOKING TIME** 0 min | **DIFFICULTY** Easy

DESCRIPTION
A cool, hydrating soup perfect for hot days, featuring juicy watermelon blended with hints of mint and lime, creating a light and invigorating dish.

INGREDIENTS

- 2 cups cubed seedless watermelon
- 1/4 cup fresh mint leaves
- Juice of 1 lime
- Optional: a pinch of chili powder or black pepper for a kick

DIRECTIONS

1. In a blender, combine watermelon, mint leaves, and lime juice. Blend until smooth.
2. If desired, season with a pinch of chili powder or black pepper.
3. Chill in the refrigerator for at least one hour.
4. Serve cold, garnished with additional mint leaves.

DIETARY INFO

Calories	80	Carbs	20g
Fat	0g	protein	1g
Fiber	1g		

0 Point Weight Loss Cookbook for Beginners

Banana Bread

SERVINGS: 1
PREP. TIME: 15 min
COOKING TIME: 45 min
DIFFICULTY: Easy

DESCRIPTION
A healthier version of traditional banana bread, made with whole ingredients and natural sweeteners, perfect for a guilt-free treat.

INGREDIENTS

- 3 ripe bananas, mashed
- 1 cup whole wheat flour
- 2 eggs
- 1/4 cup unsweetened applesauce
- 1 tsp vanilla extract
- 1 tsp baking soda
- 1/2 tsp salt
- Optional: cinnamon or nutmeg for added flavor

DIRECTIONS

1. Preheat your oven to 350°F (175°C). Grease a loaf pan.
2. In a large bowl, combine mashed bananas, eggs, applesauce, and vanilla extract.
3. In another bowl, whisk together flour, baking soda, salt, and optional spices.
4. Fold the dry ingredients into the wet ingredients until just combined.
5. Fill the loaf pan with the batter.
6. Bake for 45 minutes, or until a toothpick inserted into the center comes out clean.
7. Let cool before slicing.

DIETARY INFO

- Calories: 120
- Fat: 1g
- Fiber: 3g
- Carbs: 25g
- protein: 3g

0 Point Weight Loss Cookbook for Beginners

Chocolate Chip Cookies

SERVINGS
1

PREP. TIME
10 min

COOKING TIME
15 min

DIFFICULTY
Easy

DESCRIPTION

Soft and chewy chocolate chip cookies, made lighter with healthier substitutions, allowing for a sweet treat without the guilt.

INGREDIENTS

- 1 cup almond flour
- 1/2 cup sugar-free chocolate chips
- 1/4 cup unsweetened applesauce
- 1 egg
- 1 tsp vanilla extract
- 1/2 tsp baking soda
- Pinch of salt

DIRECTIONS

1. Preheat your oven to 350°F (175°C). Put parchment paper on one side of a baking sheet.
2. In a bowl, mix all ingredients until well combined.
3. Scoop tablespoon-sized amounts of dough onto the prepared baking sheet.
4. Bake for 15 minutes or until edges are golden.
5. After a few minutes of cooling on the baking sheet, move the baked goods to a wire rack to finish cooling.

DIETARY INFO

Calories	70	Carbs	6g
Fat	5g	protein	2g
Fiber	1g		

0 Point Weight Loss Cookbook for Beginners

Banana Ice Cream

SERVINGS 1 | **PREP. TIME** 5 min | **COOKING TIME** 0 min | **DIFFICULTY** Easy

DESCRIPTION
A creamy and delightful frozen treat made with just bananas and a touch of vanilla, this Banana Ice Cream is the perfect dairy-free and sugar-free dessert.

INGREDIENTS

- 2 ripe bananas, frozen
- 1 tsp vanilla extract

DIRECTIONS

1. Chop the frozen bananas into chunks.
2. Place banana chunks and vanilla extract in a food processor or high-speed blender.
3. Blend until smooth and creamy, scraping down the sides as necessary.
4. Serve immediately for a soft-serve texture, or freeze for an additional hour for a firmer consistency.

DIETARY INFO

Calories	105	Carbs	27g
Fat	0g	protein	1g
Fiber	3g		

0 Point Weight Loss Cookbook for Beginners

Baked Cinnamon Apples

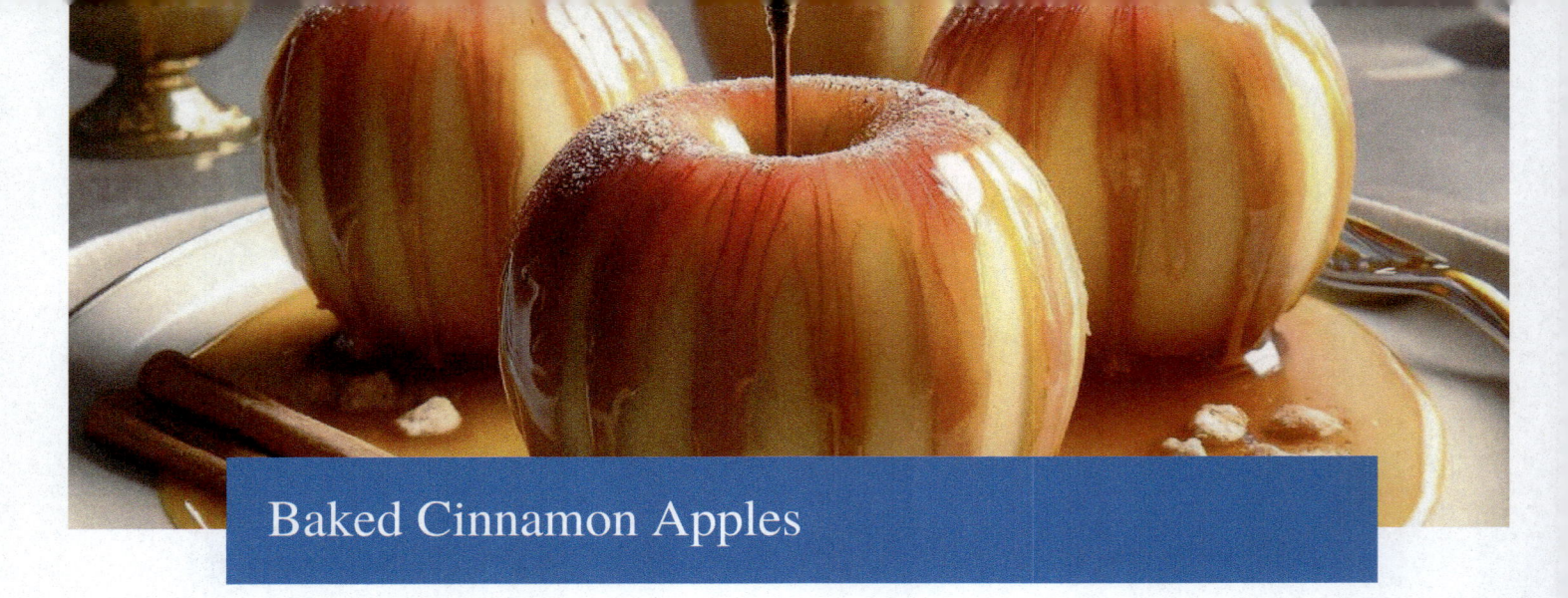

SERVINGS 1
PREP. TIME 5 min
COOKING TIME 20 min
DIFFICULTY Easy

DESCRIPTION

These Baked Cinnamon Apples are soft, sweet, and infused with the warmth of cinnamon, making them a delightful low-calorie dessert or snack.

INGREDIENTS

- 2 medium apples, cored and sliced
- 1 tsp cinnamon
- 1/4 cup water

DIRECTIONS

1. Set the oven temperature to 175°C, or 350°F.
2. Arrange apple slices in a baking dish and sprinkle with cinnamon.
3. Add water to the bottom of the dish to prevent sticking.
4. Cover with foil and bake for 20 minutes or until apples are tender.
5. Serve warm, with additional cinnamon if desired.

DIETARY INFO

Calories	9	Carbs	25g
Fat	0g	protein	0g
Fiber	5g		

Orange Segments with Cinnamon

SERVINGS	PREP. TIME	COOKING TIME	DIFFICULTY
1	5 min	0 min	Easy

DESCRIPTION

Fresh orange segments dusted with cinnamon offer a refreshing and aromatic treat, perfect for a quick snack or a light dessert.

INGREDIENTS

- 1 large orange, peeled and segmented
- 1/4 tsp cinnamon

DIRECTIONS

1. Arrange orange segments on a plate.
2. Sprinkle with cinnamon evenly over the segments.
3. For the freshest flavor, serve right away.

DIETARY INFO

Calories	62	Carbs	15g
Fat	0g	protein	1g
Fiber	3g		

Non-fat Vanilla Yogurt with Nutmeg

SERVINGS
1

PREP. TIME
5 min

COOKING TIME
0 min

DIFFICULTY
Easy

DESCRIPTION

Creamy non-fat vanilla yogurt enhanced with a hint of nutmeg creates a simple yet flavorful snack or dessert.

INGREDIENTS

- 1 cup non-fat vanilla yogurt
- 1/4 tsp ground nutmeg

DIRECTIONS

1. Spoon the yogurt into a serving bowl.
2. Sprinkle nutmeg on top of the yogurt.
3. Stir to combine, or leave layered for a visual and flavor contrast.
4. Serve chilled.

DIETARY INFO

Calories	110	Carbs	19g
Fat	0g	protein	9g
Fiber	0g		

0 Point Weight Loss Cookbook for Beginners

Peaches with Cinnamon

SERVINGS
1

PREP. TIME
5 min

COOKING TIME
0 min

DIFFICULTY
Easy

DESCRIPTION

Juicy peaches sprinkled with cinnamon are not only a delicious treat but also a healthful way to satisfy your sweet tooth.

INGREDIENTS

- 1 large peach, sliced
- 1/4 tsp cinnamon

DIRECTIONS

1. Arrange peach slices on a plate.
2. Sprinkle with cinnamon.
3. Serve fresh or chill in the refrigerator before serving for a refreshing snack.

DIETARY INFO

	Calories	68		Carbs	17g
	Fat	0g		protein	1g
	Fiber	3g			

0 Point Weight Loss Cookbook for Beginners

No Sugar Less Ghee Churma Ladoo

SERVINGS 1 | **PREP. TIME** 15 min | **COOKING TIME** 20 min | **DIFFICULTY** Easy

DESCRIPTION
Churma Ladoo is a traditional Indian sweet, here modified to be healthier with less ghee and no added sugar, focusing on natural sweetness.

INGREDIENTS

- 1 cup whole wheat flour
- 2 tbsp ghee (clarified butter)
- 1/2 cup grated jaggery or date paste for natural sweetness
- 1/4 tsp cardamom powder

DIRECTIONS

1. In a pan, roast whole wheat flour on low heat with 1 tbsp ghee until golden brown.
2. Turn off the heat and let it to cool.
3. Add grated jaggery or date paste and cardamom powder. Mix well.
4. Form into small balls (ladoos) using your hands. If the mixture is too dry, add a little warm milk or the remaining ghee to bind.
5. Store in an airtight container or serve at room temperature.

DIETARY INFO

Calories	150	Carbs	22g
Fat	6g	protein	2g
Fiber	2g		

0 Point Weight Loss Cookbook for Beginners

Fruit Salad with Mint

SERVINGS 1 | **PREP. TIME** 10 min | **COOKING TIME** 0 min | **DIFFICULTY** Easy

DESCRIPTION

A refreshing and colorful mix of fruits enhanced with fresh mint, perfect for a light dessert or a vibrant start to your day.

INGREDIENTS

- 1/2 cup sliced strawberries
- 1/2 cup cubed watermelon
- 1/2 cup cubed pineapple
- 1/4 cup blueberries
- 2 tablespoons chopped fresh mint

DIRECTIONS

1. In a large bowl, combine strawberries, watermelon, pineapple, and blueberries.
2. Sprinkle chopped mint over the fruit.
3. Toss gently to combine. Serve immediately or chill to enhance the flavors.

DIETARY INFO

- Calories 100
- Carbs 25g
- Fat 1g
- Protein 1g
- Fiber 3g

Poached Pears

SERVINGS 1 | **PREP. TIME** 5 min | **COOKING TIME** 25 min | **DIFFICULTY** Easy

DESCRIPTION
Elegant and simple, these poached pears are cooked gently in a spiced syrup, making them a perfect low-calorie dessert.

INGREDIENTS

- 1 large pear, peeled, halved, and cored
- 2 cups water
- 1/4 cup honey or a sweetener of choice
- 1 cinnamon stick
- 1 star anise

DIRECTIONS

1. In a saucepan large enough to hold the pear halves, combine water, honey, cinnamon, and star anise. Bring to a simmer.
2. Add the pear halves. Simmer gently for 25 minutes, or until the pears are tender.
3. Remove the pears and increase the heat to reduce the liquid to a thick syrup.
4. Serve the pears with a drizzle of the reduced syrup.

DIETARY INFO

Calories	120	Carbs	30g
Fat	0g	protein	1g
Fiber	5g		

Healthy Homemade Snack Bar

SERVINGS
1

PREP. TIME
15 min

COOKING TIME
0 min

DIFFICULTY
Easy

DESCRIPTION

These no-bake snack bars are packed with nuts, seeds, and dried fruits, offering a healthy energy boost.

INGREDIENTS

- 1/2 cup rolled oats
- 1/4 cup chopped almonds
- 1/4 cup dried cranberries
- 1/4 cup pumpkin seeds
- 1/4 cup honey or agave syrup
- 1/4 cup peanut butter

DIRECTIONS

1. In a bowl, thoroughly mix all ingredients.
2. Press the mixture into a lined square dish.
3. Refrigerate for at least 2 hours or until firm.
4. Cut into bars and serve. Store remaining bars in an airtight container in the refrigerator.

DIETARY INFO

Calories	200	Carbs	25g
Fat	10g	protein	6g
Fiber	4g		

No Sugar No Jaggery Dry Fruit Roll

SERVINGS 1 | **PREP. TIME** 10 min | **COOKING TIME** 0 min | **DIFFICULTY** Easy

DESCRIPTION
A delightful roll made entirely of nuts and dried fruits, compressed into a dense, sweet treat without any added sugars or sweeteners.

INGREDIENTS

- 1/2 cup dates, pitted
- 1/4 cup figs
- 1/4 cup raisins
- 1/4 cup cashews
- 1/4 cup almonds

DIRECTIONS

1. In a food processor, combine dates, figs, raisins, cashews, and almonds. Process until the mixture forms a sticky dough.
2. Lay the mixture on a piece of parchment paper and roll it into a log shape.
3. Chill in the refrigerator for a few hours until firm.
4. Slice into rounds and serve.

DIETARY INFO

Calories	150	Carbs	18g
Fat	8g	protein	3g
Fiber	2g		

No Atta Banana Halwa

SERVINGS	PREP. TIME	COOKING TIME	DIFFICULTY
1	5 min	15 min	Easy

DESCRIPTION
A unique and simple dessert, this banana halwa is made without wheat flour, relying on the natural sweetness and texture of bananas.

INGREDIENTS

- 2 ripe bananas, mashed
- 1 tablespoon ghee
- 1/2 teaspoon cardamom powder

DIRECTIONS

1. In a non-stick skillet, heat ghee over medium heat.
2. Add mashed bananas and cardamom powder. Cook, stirring constantly, until the mixture thickens and starts leaving the sides of the pan (about 15 minutes).
3. Serve warm or let it cool and set in a dish, then cut into squares.

DIETARY INFO

Calories	180	Carbs	30g
Fat	7g	protein	1g
Fiber	3g		

0 Point Weight Loss Cookbook for Beginners

Conclusion

Congratulations on your commitment from the very first page to this one. I believe this book has positively impacted your lifestyle, especially in terms of health.

Embracing the 0 Point Diet is more than a culinary journey; it's a transformative lifestyle change that emphasizes health, well-being, and mindful eating. By focusing on zero-point foods—those rich in nutrients but low in calories—you've taken significant steps toward enhancing your overall health. This diet isn't just about weight loss; it's about learning to make sustainable, healthful choices that nourish your body and satiate your palate.

The recipes and meal plans provided in this guide are designed to introduce you to a world where dieting doesn't mean deprivation. Instead, it's a delightful exploration of flavors and ingredients that promote a healthy lifestyle. The 0 Point Diet underscores the importance of whole, unprocessed foods, which are crucial for long-term health and well-being. These foods help reduce the risk of chronic diseases, maintain energy levels, and support overall body function.

As you continue on this path, remember that every meal is an opportunity to positively impact your health. I encourage you to keep experimenting with new ingredients and recipes.

Thank you so much.

Your Bonus is here

I would like to thank you a lot, first and foremost, for picking up this book, and secondly, for dedicating your time to practice the recipes. Get you bonus in the next page—enjoy!

28-Day Meal Plan

Note: All Recipes listed below are covered in the book

Week 1

Day 1
- B Flourless Banana Pancakes
- M Grilled Chicken Salad
- D Slow Cooker Chicken Fajita Soup

Day 2
- B Easy Cheeseburger Pie
- M Two-ingredient Dough
- D Baked Cod with Tomato and Basil

Day 3
- B Bundt Cake Breakfast
- M Spicy Black Bean Soup
- D Chinese Chicken Salad

Day 4
- B Bacon and Egg Cucumber Bites
- M Cauliflower Steak
- D Fish Taco Bowls

Day 5
- B Pineapple Coconut Oatmeal Muffins
- M Zucchini and Carrot Noodles
- D Mushroom Stroganoff

Day 6
- B Smoked Salmon and Cucumber Rolls
- M Caesar Salad
- D Chicken Taco Casserole

Day 7
- B WW Peanut Butter Energy Balls
- M Cabbage Rolls
- D Quiche

Week 2

Day 8
- B Egg Muffins
- M Eggplant and Tomato Layer Bake
- D Spaghetti Squash Lasagna

Day 9
- B 2-Minute Omelet in a Mug
- M Roasted Mixed Vegetables
- D Portobello Mushroom Pizzas

Day 10
- B Hard-Boiled Eggs and Asparagus
- M Chicken Salad
- D Baked Chicken Parmesan

Day 11
- B Apple Cinnamon Porridge
- M Chicken and Vegetable Soup
- D Beef and Vegetable Kebabs

Day 12
- B Turkey Lettuce Wraps
- M Shrimp and Asparagus Stir-Fry
- D Lemon and Herb Shrimp

Day 13
- B Crispy Air Fryer Turkey Bacon
- M Stuffed Bell Peppers
- D Mushroom Pork Chops

Day 14
- B Zucchini Noodles with Tomato Sauce
- M Herb-Crusted Pork Tenderloin
- D Baked Garlic Lemon Salmon

Week 3

Day 15
- B: French Toast ()
- M: Balsamic Glazed Brussels Sprouts
- D: Baked Buffalo Chicken Taquitos

Day 16
- B: Cauliflower Rice Porridge
- M: Chicken Piccata
- D: Chicken Quesadillas

Day 17
- B: Pumpkin Banana Greek Yogurt Muffins
- M: Beef & Bean Chili
- D: Chickpea and Feta Salad

Day 18
- B: Burrito Bowl with Spiced Butternut Squash
- L: Spaghetti Squash with Marinara
- D: Southwest Chicken Salad

Day 19
- B: Grilled Eggplant and Tomato Stack
- M: Tuna and White Bean Salad
- D: Balsamic Vinegar Chicken

Day 20
- B: Instant Pot Egg Bake
- M: Super-easy Slow-Cooker Three-Bean Chili
- D: Mexican Zero Point Soup

Day 21
- B: Flourless Banana Pancakes
- L: Vegetable Soup
- D: Slow Cooker Chicken Fajita Soup

Week 4

Day 22
- B: Easy Cheeseburger Pie
- M: Zucchini Noodle Caprese
- D: Chinese Chicken Salad

Day 23
- B: Bundt Cake Breakfast
- M: Easy Fried Rice
- D: Fish Taco Bowls

Day 24
- B: Bacon and Egg Cucumber Bites
- M: Grilled Cheddar Cheese Sandwiches
- D: Mushroom Stroganoff

Day 25
- B: Pineapple Coconut Oatmeal Muffins
- M: Tomato Basil Soup
- D: Chicken Taco Casserole

Day 26
- B: Smoked Salmon and Cucumber Rolls
- M: Broccoli & Cheddar Quiche
- D: Quiche

Day 27
- B: WW Peanut Butter Energy Balls
- M: Grilled Summer Vegetables
- D: Spaghetti Squash Lasagna

Day 28
- B: Egg Muffins
- M: Fresh Vegetable Soup
- D: Portobello Mushroom Pizzas

Notes:

B denote Breakfast
M denote Main Course
D denote Dinner

Measurement Conversions

Weight Equivalents

US Standards	Metric (Approximates)
1/2 Ounce	15g
1 Ounce	30g
2 Ounces	60g
4 Ounces	115g
8 Ounces	225g
12 Ounces	340g
16 Ounces	455g

Oven Temperatures

Fahrenheit (F)	Celsius(C) (Approximates)
250 F	120 C
300 F	150 C
325 F	165 C
350 F	180 C
375 F	190 C
400 F	200 C
425 F	220 C
450 F	230 C

Volume Equivalents (Liquid)

US Standards	US Standard (ounce)	Metric (approximate)
2 tablespoons	1 fl. oz.	30 ml
1/4 cup	2 fl. oz.	60 ml
1/2 cup	4 fl. oz.	120 ml
1 cup	8 fl. oz.	240 ml
1 1/2 cup	12 fl. oz.	355 ml
2 cups or 1 pint	16 fl. oz.	475 ml
4 cups or 1 quart	32 fl. oz.	1 L
1 gallon	128 fl. oz.	4 L

Volume Equivalents (Dry)

US Standards	Metric (approximate)	US Standards	Metric (approximate)
1/4 teaspoon	0.5 ml	1/3 cup	79 ml
1/4 teaspoon	1 ml	1/2 cup	118 ml
1/2 teaspoon	4 ml	2/3 cup	156 ml
1 teaspoon	5 ml	3/4 cup	177 ml
1 tablespoon	15 ml	1 cup	235 ml
1/4 cup	59 ml	2 cups or 1 pint	475 ml

Printed in Great Britain
by Amazon